John's Miracles
Seeing Beyond Our Expectations

Phillip A. Ross

Marietta, Ohio

Copyright ©2019 Phillip A. Ross
All rights reserved.

ISBN: 978-1-7337267-0-2
Edition: 2019.9.10

Published by
Pilgrim Platform
149 E. Spring St., Marietta
Ohio, 45750
www.pilgrim-platform.org

Unless otherwise indicated Scripture has been taken from The Holy Bible, New King James Version ©1982 by Thomas Nelson, Inc.

Printed in the United States of America

The cover design includes a classic optical illusion that you probably won't notice unless it is pointed out.

> "... I have come into this world,
> so that the blind will see
> and those who see will become blind."
> —John 9:39

> "Whether individual or collective, willful blindness doesn't have a single driver, but many. It is a human phenomenon to which we all succumb in matters little and large. We can't notice and know everything: the cognitive limits of our brain simply won't let us. That means we have to filter or edit what we take in. So what we choose to let through and to leave out is crucial. We mostly admit the information that makes us feel great about ourselves, while conveniently filtering whatever unsettles our fragile egos and most vital beliefs."
> —Margaret Heffernan

Books by Phillip A. Ross

The Work At Zion—A Reckoning, Two-volume set, 772 pages, 1996.
Practically Christian—Applying James Today, 135 pages, 2006.
The Wisdom of Jesus Christ in the Book of Proverbs, 414 pages, 2006.
Marking God's Word—Understanding Jesus, 324 pages, 2006.
Acts of Faith—Kingdom Advancement, 326 pages, 2007.
Informal Christianity—Refining Christ's Church, 136 pages, 2007.
Engagement—Establishing Relationship in Christ, 104 pages, 1996, 2008.
It's About Time! — The Time Is Now, 40 pages. 2008.
The Big Ten—A Study of the Ten Commandments, 105 pages, 2001, 2008.
Arsy Varsy—Reclaiming The Gospel in First Corinthians, 406 pages, 2008.
Varsy Arsy—Proclaiming The Gospel in Second Corinthians, 356 pages, 2009.
Colossians—Christos Singularis, 278 pages, 2010.
Rock Mountain Creed—The Sermon on the Mount, 310 pages, 2011.
The True Mystery of the Mystical Presence, 355 pages, 2011.
Peter's Vision of Christ's Purpose in First Peter, 340 pages, 2011.
Peter's Vision of The End in Second Peter, 184 pages, 2012.
The Religious History of Nineteenth Century Marietta, Thomas Jefferson Summers, 124 pages, 1903, 2012 (editor).
Conflict of Ages—The Great Debate of the Moral Relations of God and Man, Edward Beecher, 489 pages, 1853, 2012 (editor).
Concord Of Ages—The Individual And Organic Harmony Of God And Man, Edward Beecher, D. D., 524 pages, 1860, 2013 (editor).
Ephesians—Recovering the Vision of a Sustainable Church in Christ, 417 pages, 2013.
Galatians: Backstory/Christory, 315 pages, 2015.
Poet Tree—Root, Branch & Sap, 72 pages, 2013.
Inside Out Woman—Collected Poetry, Doris M. Ross, 195 pages, 2014 (editor).
God's Great Plan for the World, 305 pages, 2019.
John's Miracles—Seeing Beyond Our Expectations, 210 pages, 2019.

*For those who have
ears to ear and eyes to see
Maranatha!*

TABLE OF CONTENTS

Introduction..i

Water Into Wine
Beginning of Signs..1

The Woman At The Well
Secret Food..11
No Honor...19

The Official's Son
Healing Miracle..29

The Pool of Bethesda
Wilt Thou?...37
No More...45
Verily, Verily..53
Hear and Believe..61
Come Forth..69
Testified Of Christ..77
God's Honor...87
The Accuser...95

Food For The Hungry
The Test...105
The Source...113
The Remainder...121

Walking on Water
One Night On The Sea...131
The Works of God..139
What Sign?...147
Bread From Heaven...157
God's Will...165

Born Blind
Spit & Dirt..175

Resurrection
Lazarus: Dead and Alive..185

INTRODUCTION

Signs and wonders is the catch phrase for the renewed interest in miraculous phenomena of the past several decades. The meteoric rise of charismatic and Pentecostal churches throughout the world suggests a renewed seriousness in miracles and miraculous phenomena.

The study before you began as a expositional preaching series on the gospel of John in the mid-1990s in Evansville, Indiana. Rightly or wrongly, the first chapter of John was not treated because of the excessive familiarity with it on the part of most church attending people. It is a favorite Christmas reading, and my beginning point for this series was not Christmas. So I skipped it.

As I delved deeper into John's gospel it became increasingly clear to me that John had a unique perspective regarding the miracles of Jesus. It was not long before this exposition of John began to take on a life of its own. A pattern emerged regarding John's treatment of Jesus' miracles that suggested a significant departure from anything I have read in various commentaries. My commentary reading is far from exhaustive, but it is representative of the Mainline and Reformed perspectives.

The perspective that emerged suggested that John's concern for holding in tension the humanity and divinity of Christ was also reflected in his treatment of Jesus' miracles. Being the last gospel written, John seemed to offer a correction or at least an additional perspective regarding the normal, almost magical and supernatural understanding that has been attached to the miracles of the Lord. As a counterbalance John offers a consistent perspective that avails itself of various naturalistic interpretations of the miracles, but doesn't stop there. John makes the case that many of Jesus' miracles may involve sufficient natural explanations that might counter the usual miraculous or magical understanding.

But John was not content to leave the matter of miracles in the hands of naturalists. Thank God! By and large the liberal wing of the modern church has latched onto naturalistic interpretations of Jesus' miracles—and that exclusively—to the point that the supernatural has been eliminated from the liberal perspective. However, the elimination of the supernatural was not what John was up to. John did not eliminate the supernatural. Rather, he put it into perspective by making a much more convincing case for the reality of the supernatural by frankly admitting that many of the miracles could just as well have naturalistic explanations. To admit to some natural explanations makes the truly supernatural all the more viable by showing that your consideration is not from a wild-eyed, literalist, or fundamentalist perspective. In addition, such an admission shifts the locus of the miraculous, and opens new vistas of spirituality for exploration.

The perspective of these pages may take some getting used to, so I beg your patience. Don't dismiss what you think I'm trying to say before you understand it.[1] Rather, allow me to put my perspective on the table for your inspection and hopefully you will find that, while a pre-Modern, simplistic and magical perspective dissolves in the light of science and a plain Modern reading of the text, a more genuine and meaningful perspective arises when you don't simply dismiss Scripture as nonsense, but continue to trust that it is true. To hold on to the veracity of the Bible requires understanding how what it says can be true. Premature judgment will short-circuit the process.

John draws those with a naturalistic bent into his gospel by granting to them certain clarifications of the synoptic gospel stories about various miracles that provide for a naturalistic interpretation, even by first century standards. By doing so he also eliminates certain naturalistic explanations that will not hold up to closer scrutiny. The consequence of this is that John redefines and reintroduces the super-

---

[1] One of my favorite quotes: "I know that you believe you understand what you think I said, but I'm not sure you realize that what you heard is not what I meant" — Robert McCloskey.

natural in a much deeper and more convincing manner. By allowing certain naturalistic explanations he also disallows the dismissal of genuinely supernatural elements and evidence.

John holds in tension the natural and the supernatural in his treatment of miracles because he holds Jesus' humanity and divinity in tension. His treatment of the humanity and divinity of Christ is reflected in his handling of the natural and supernatural elements of Jesus' miracles. John grants much more latitude to the naturalists than traditional Christians are comfortable with. So, as you read please be patient and careful in your study. Assume the scientific attitude. Don't dismiss what you think you know about the world to be scientifically true. Look for the evidence of naturalistic explanations, and grant them the courtesy of consideration. But don't stop there.

Don't abandon belief in the reality of God's supernatural intervention into both nature and history. Be patient and careful in your reading, generous in your interpretation, and be ready to be surprised by God's intervention into your own perspective. After all, this is the purpose of the Bible.

I am deeply appreciative to my wife, Stephanie, who has endured my probing into traditionally established Christians explanations and yet continued to trust the Holy Spirit's guidance in matters close to her heart. A finer helpmeet could not be found.

A word of thanks also goes to Dr. James E. "Jed" Martin, who has offered critical insight and support for the first draft. The unifying theme of this study was suggested to me in a casual conversation with the Rev. Garry Sutley (State College, Pennsylvania), to whom I am grateful for enduring friendship and inestimable patience with me a Christian far removed from his own theological tradition—and who has since died. Much of what I have said in these pages has in my own mind been directed and guided by many conversations with some special friends, Angela Keene and Linda Brawley included.

May God grant the blessings of His Holy Spirit to accompany the reading and study of what follows. I pray that the Lord use it in whatever way He best sees fit, for it is His. To Him belongs whatever glory it may accrue.

Phillip A. Ross
Zion, Pennsylvania
1996

Introduction II

Coming back to this study after some fifteen years I was impressed with some of the insights in it, and unhappy with others. Consequently, much of this material has been edited and reworked to incorporate my continuing growth in grace and discernment. It is important for readers to understand that, while Scripture provides a fixed point from which to correctly view and analyze our world and its philosophy, history, etc., one's own perspective continues to grow and mature over time. Growth and maturity are only seen in reference to a previous point of development. Thus, at this point my concern for this study of John's view of Christ's miracles is to preserve what is of value, to correct its shortcomings, to improve both the writing and the analysis, and to extend this examination further into the gospel of John. The original study began at the Cana wedding in chapter three and didn't quite finish with Jesus walking on the water in chapter six.

The insight that is most worth preserving and refining is that John has provided both a natural and a supernatural clarification and explanation for Christ's miracles that corresponds to Christ's dual nature as fully man and fully God, which itself issues from biblical Trinitarianism. We should not be surprised that Christ would do various things that can be seen and understood from both a human and a divine (or a natural and a supernatural) perspective. This is not to suggest that I or anyone else have access to the fullness of God's divine perspective. Though, again, it needs to be understood that one of the primary purposes of Scripture itself is to provide some access to God's perspective, with the process of regeneration expanding that perspective further—yet stopping significantly short of God's comprehensive perspective. So, while we cannot understand God's perspective fully, we can understand it sufficiently through the power and presence of the Holy Spirit through regeneration. We can understand God well enough to meet our own personal needs and desires for spiritual maturity. Indeed, Christ's mission in coming to earth is to provide additional access to God, and to reveal more of God's purpose than was available in the Old Testament.

Marietta, Ohio
2008

Introduction III

This manuscript has remained unpublished for another decade because I knew that it was unfinished, but didn't quite know what to do to finish it. It was never intended to include all of the miracles in the gospel of John, but it needed something more. My most recent writing project (*God's Great Mission for the World*, 2019) caused me to include three chapters of this manuscript as an appendix because it provided some background or foundation for some of the ideas pursued in *God's Great Mission*. So, I reviewed this manuscript again.

My friend Ray V. Foss and I have been spending much time together and working on various projects together, and at some point he shared with me his understanding of the three uses of God's law. There is nothing new about this idea, but Ray has a creative way of discussing and illustrating the issue.

The first use of the law (curb) he calls "rumble strips." On our highways rumble strips are etched into the sides of the highway, and when one encounters them at high speed they make a loud noise, which alerts you to the fact that you are at the limit of the road and need to recenter your driving. The law helps to curb certain behaviors.

He describes the second use of the law (mirror) as a "signal mirror." One can use it to show yourself up (see your own reflection) or you can signal your location (use the sun's reflection to reveal your location to someone else by flashing reflected sunlight at them). The law reveals our sin, and shows us to be sinners to others.

The third use of the law (guide) he refers to as "spit and dirt," a reference to Jesus' healing of the man born blind in John 9. Here God's law is used as a guide for better living, where "better" is understood as moral improvement. The law can be used to further our sanctification.

In working on another project with Ray Foss dealing with Jesus' healing of the man born blind I realized that I needed to include that story here. So I have. But that healing also leads directly into the raising of Lazarus. So I included that one, too. And by adding these two miracles in the gospel of John I found this manuscript to have arrived at completion. As a consequence, I omitted the chapters in the appendix of *God's Great Plan*, and refer readers to this now completed book.

Consequently, one of my earliest manuscripts (this one) and my most recent (*God's Great Plan*) will be published at the same time. Both of these books may be difficult for Christians to understand today because the condition of the churches in the early twenty-first century is pretty dismal. Understandably so, because there is so much being written from so many divergent perspectives that it is difficult to deal with. Much good theology is being done, but much bad theology is also being done. Most Christians realize that we are in need of revival or reformation, which means that the church in our day is pretty ineffective.

These are truly confusing times for Christians. Most people simply give up reading the Bible, and don't read much theology, and those who do read, don't usually read outside of their own traditions. Consequently, Christianity has clarified itself into two main divisions (conservative and liberal) with a thousand splinters branching off each node. As an American I recognize that these two factions have been struggling on this continent for prominence since before America was founded in 1776. And that struggle is coming to some kind of head in the twenty-first century. American politics and religion are as fractious as they have ever been, probably more so!

I'm a bit of an anomaly among Christians today because I grew up as a liberal and all of my studies (B.A. in philosophy and M.Div.) have been on the liberal wing. But in the early 1980s the Lord grabbed me by the nape of the neck, and I've never been the same. I renounced my liberal education and have been reeducating myself ever since. I now identify as a conservative, born-again Christian, but I'm not a fundamentalist or a biblical literalist. I'm adamantly Reformed, but I believe that God's miraculous gifts will never cease. I identify as a charismatic because I believe that God's *charis* (grace) is foundational, but not automatic. I believe in speaking in tongues, but have a very different understanding of what that means than my charismatic friends.[2] I believe in both God's predestination of all things, and in the free will of human beings, and that these two per-

---

2 My understanding of tongues can be found in *Arsy Varsy—Reclaiming The Gospel in First Corinthians*, Pilgrim Platform, Marietta, Ohio, 2008.

spectives must be held together, much as Jesus' divinity and His humanity.

I offer this book, as I offer all of my books, for the edification of Christians and nonChristians alike. I believe that my work provides a perspective on the Bible and on Christianity that has merit. But I'm not offering a new kind of Christianity, nor a new perspective on the Bible. Rather, my perspective is that of renewal, of revival, and hopefully of reformation. But I'm not looking back to the sixteenth century, nor the twelfth, nor the twentieth. Rather, I'm looking ahead to the future, to the kingdom that God has been anticipating for some time. Entry into that kingdom will not require the abandonment of the past. Rather, it will provide a perspective from which humanity's past can be both seriously appreciated, carefully critiqued, lovingly embraced, and transcended—not forgotten, but built upon. But that is not for me to judge.

Special thanks to my wife, Stephanie, for proofreading.

Marietta, Ohio
2019

WATER INTO WINE

Beginning of Signs

"Philip found Nathanael and said to him, 'We have found him of whom Moses in the Law and also the prophets wrote, Jesus of Nazareth, the son of Joseph.' Nathanael said to him, 'Can anything good come out of Nazareth?' Philip said to him, 'Come and see.' Jesus saw Nathanael coming toward him and said of him, 'Behold, an Israelite indeed, in whom there is no deceit!' Nathanael said to him, 'How do you know me?' Jesus answered him, 'Before Philip called you, when you were under the fig tree, I saw you.' Nathanael answered him, 'Rabbi, you are the Son of God! You are the King of Israel!' Jesus answered him, 'Because I said to you, "I saw you under the fig tree," do you believe? You will see greater things than these.' And he said to him, 'Truly, truly, I say to you, you will see heaven opened, and the angels of God ascending and descending on the Son of Man.'

On the third day there was a wedding at Cana in Galilee, and the mother of Jesus was there. Jesus also was invited to the wedding with his disciples. When the wine ran out, the mother of Jesus said to him, 'They have no wine.' And Jesus said to her, 'Woman, what does this have to do with me? My hour has not yet come.' His mother said to the servants, 'Do whatever he tells you.' Now there were six stone water jars there for the Jewish rites of purification, each holding twenty or thirty gallons. Jesus said to the servants, "Fill the *jars with water.' And they filled them up to the brim. And he said to them, 'Now draw some out and take it to the master of the feast.' So they took it. When the master of the feast tasted the water now become wine, and did not know where it came from (though the servants who had drawn the water knew), the master of the feast called the bridegroom and said to him, 'Everyone serves the good wine first, and when people have drunk freely, then the poor wine. But you have kept the good wine until now.' This, the first of his signs, Jesus did at Cana in Galilee, and manifested his glory. And his disciples believed in him.* —John 1:45-2:1-11

It is important to note the last few verses of chapter one because of the promises made to Jesus' disciples. As an aside, note that Jesus told His disciples that they would have better reasons to believe than Nathanael's superstitious remark that he believed because Jesus "*saw* (him) under the fig tree" (John 1:50). Jesus may have been correcting a superstitious belief akin to the Hindu *darśana*,[1] a mystical connection forged between a Hindu guru (considered to be a god) and his disciple through a mutual "seeing" of one another. Part of the thesis of this book is that Jesus came to correct and dispel various ancient and tenacious religious superstitions that had wormed their way into Old Testament Judaism of His time. We know that there had been very early contact between ancient Israel and ancient India.[2] Israel has always been at the crossroads of world trade, and Old Testament Israel had much contact with various pagan religions.

Jesus would shortly provide much evidence for His disciples to believe the gospel, as we will see. In verse 51 Jesus promised some grand signs or miracles. We know that because He began with a double *amen* (the ESV translates it as *truly*). The double *amen* (or *truly*), a literary device found only in the gospel of John and which

---

1   Darśana is commonly used for theophany or a manifestation or vision of the divine. In Hindu worship, e.g. of a deity (especially in image form), or a very holy person or artifact. One can receive darśana or a glimpse of the deity in the temple, or from a great saintly person, such as a great guru. Hinduism is a very old religion, and perhaps something like this existed elsewhere. The similarities are noteworthy.
2   https://wiki2.org/en/Hinduism_and_Judaism

appears some fifty-one times, is a means that John uses to alert readers to the fact that what follows is very important. So we need to be on the lookout for them.

Most commentators agree that verse 51 is an allusion to Jacob's ladder, referred to in Genesis 28:12. The argument is that the ladder, representing a connection between heaven and earth, was broken by the sin of Adam, and will be restored by the return of Christ at His second coming. It denotes a type of gospel restoration in the cosmos. Although this is the literal gist of what Jesus said, we know from the fact that He is about to perform His first miracle that His words in some degree pointed to the fact that the disciples were about to witness miracles. And in the Old Testament miracles were given to establish the credentials or credibility of a prophet, one who spoke God's truth.

We would do well to pause and consider the nature of the miracles that we will examine here and elsewhere in John. A few introductory remarks will help. John employs a particular language or phrasing when referring to Jesus' miracles. There are two primary Greek words for miracle: *dunamis* (δύναμις) and *semeion* (σημεῖον).

> "The Synoptists use *dunamis*, not *semeion*, for the miracles of Jesus, and it is these *dunamis* (which opponents attribute to sorcery) that prompt the demand for a sign."[3]

John only uses *semeion*, which suggests a particular viewpoint that opposes sorcery. It is my thesis in this book that one of the reasons that John wrote his gospel was to correct some previous misunderstandings that had arisen regarding Jesus' miracles. Misunderstanding Jesus was a common phenomenon from the very beginning.[4]

In describing the synoptic use of *semeion* Bromley says that such a miracle does not have to be a miraculous or apocalyptic sign, whereas *dunamis* was often thought of in terms of magic by those who heard Jesus speak. In itself *semeion* simply makes the divine

---

3   *Theological Dictionary of the New Testament*, Geoffrey W. Bromiley, Eerdmans, Grand Rapids, Michigan, p. 1019. The "synoptists" refers to Matthew, Mark and Luke.
4   *Marking God's Word—Understanding Jesus*, Phillip A. Ross, Pilgrim Platform, Marietta, Ohio, 2006.

presence recognizable. A *semeion* does not need to be miraculous itself, rather it simply points to a miracle.

> "On the one side *semeion* occurs with verbs that denote human activity or that objectify it so that one can ask for it, see it, or accept or deny it. On the other side it is from heaven or from God. ...what is signified is beyond human competence but comes into the human sphere by means of the *semeion*. When a *semeion* occurs in the NT, humans are always involved and there is a pointer to human responsibility...."[5]

My thesis is that John's treatment of miracles is an attempt to hold the divinity and humanity of Christ in creative tension, not as a literary device but because that is the reality of Christ's two natures—the human and the divine. The dual nature of Christ requires that we understand His miracles, and everything He did, from a dual nature perspective as well. John treats Christ's miracles as both human and divine occurrences. To say that miracles are rooted in human experience or in nature is only an acknowledgment that existence itself is ultimately miraculous. It is the acknowledgment that nature is not free from God's control, as if God and nature are opposed to one another. They are not.

However, to overemphasize the naturalistic elements of Christ's miracles portrays Him as a clever opportunist who manipulates people and situations to serve His own ends. On the other hand, to overemphasize supernaturalism is to present Him as a magician. Christ was neither. Thus, determining or seeing the correct balance between His divinity and His humanity is critical. We will find that this dual perspective of Christ's miracles actually reveals deeper and more subtle dimensions of the miraculous that are more difficult to dismiss because they are more real, especially in the light of Modern science.

John's intention was to present the truth of Christ's humanity and His divinity as it was reflected in who He was and what He did. This tension is also embedded in the miracles He wrought. John reveals the divine presence in the human Christ. In doing so he offers the proof of Jesus' signs or miracles (*semeion*) that point to the presence of the divine that has broken into the world *through* the human person of Jesus Christ. Just as Christ the Lord is revealed through and

---

5   Ibid., Bromiley, p. 1018.

in Jesus the man, Christ's miracles reveal God through and in the activities of Jesus the man. The miracle at the wedding at Cana of Galilee is such a pointer (*semeion*).

Mother Mary

Jesus was raised in Galilee, and it was quite natural that He and his Galilean disciples would attend a wedding in Cana because they had friends in the area. The fact that they ran out of wine suggests the relative poverty of the families involved. Wealthier families would not have had such a problem. This substantiates the traditional understanding that Jesus' family was poor and that He associated with the poor.

We can only speculate as to why Mary went to Jesus saying, "They have no wine" (v. 3). It is easily supposed that she asked Him to produce wine, but that is not what is recorded in the text. She simply stated the case. There may have been the implication by tone or idiom that she indeed wanted Jesus to correct the situation. Perhaps she hoped that He would go to the market and purchase more wine for the festivities. Again, this is only speculation.

At this point she had no reason to suspect that Jesus could or would perform a miracle. She had no reason to suppose that He could, even if He wanted to, miraculously manufacture wine from water. Jesus had performed no miracles to date. Yet, Mary had treasured in her heart many things about her son Jesus. The shepherds had prophesied His birth. And Simeon and Anna had prophesied mysterious things about Him at His circumcision (Luke 2:21-38). Mary had reason to suspect something special about her son, but as far as we know she had no hard facts. Nonetheless, she said to Him, "They have no wine." And Jesus said to her, "Woman, what does this have to do with me? My hour has not yet come" (John 2:3-4).

At first sight Jesus' response seems unnecessarily harsh. Our reaction may be the result of our own cultural experience as much as anything. The appellation "woman" coming from the mouth of a son to his mother sounds cold to our modern ears. We forget that Jesus addressed Mary in the same way when He was on the cross, affectionately telling her to look to John to care for her (John 20:15). Nonetheless, calling your mother "woman" sounds pretty cold today.

In essence, Jesus told Mary that her concern for wine at the wedding had nothing to do with His ministry, suggesting that since His public ministry had just begun (with His baptism—(John 1:29–33, compare: Matthew 3:13–17; Mark 1:9–11; Luke 3:21–23) He must only be involved in the work of His ministry, and had nothing to do with this wedding. He might well have been concerned that from that point forward people would look at everything that He did, as if he was a public figure. And so He may have thought that He should only do what was necessary for His ministry.

His comment about "My hour has not yet come" (v. 4) certainly strengthens this understanding. All of the events of His short, public ministry must serve the purpose God had given Him. Jesus seems to indicate that He will have nothing to do with the wine problem. And yet He didn't say He wouldn't do something about it. To add to the confusion, after saying it had nothing to do with Him, he worked the miracle. Go figure!

Mary left the situation in His hands. She told the wedding servants to do whatever (if anything) Jesus told them to do. That is generally good advice for all Christians: do what the Lords says to do. It is, in fact, the key to biblical understanding. Understanding of the Scriptures will be greatly enhanced by obedience. And conversely, disobedience will close the Scriptures to one's understanding.

The Pots

John noted six stone water pots, but didn't say whether they were empty or full. Since the wedding party had been going on for some time, we must assume that some of them would have been partly full at that point. Surely some of the water had been used. John noted that the pots each held twenty to thirty gallons. So, altogether that would be one hundred and twenty to one hundred and eighty gallons of water in all six pots.

In order to fill the pots someone had to go get at least fifty-or-so gallons of water. A fair amount of time and energy would have been required to fill them. Yet, no mention of this was made in the text. Regardless, Jesus told the wedding servants to fill the pots with water. That is, to make sure that they were all full to the brim with water. Why add this detail? With the pots full of water, we can be sure that nothing else had been added to produce the wine. They were simply filled to the brim with water.

Once they were filled Jesus instructed them to go back and draw some (presumably water) out of the pots—pots that they themselves had just filled to the top with water—and take it to the master of the feast. At this point the master of the feast was not aware of what Jesus had done. No one was. So the master of the feast provided an objective, unbiased estimate of the miracle because he was completely unaware of Mary's request or Jesus' activity. No previous mention of him had been made. He tasted the cup—no longer water, but now wine—and responded that it was the best wine of the wedding party.

He commented to the groom that the normal custom of serving the best wine first had been reversed. The reversal of the normal is a key part of what God was doing through Jesus' ministry. Again, the Second Temple culture had been infected with various superstitions and ungodly practices that needed to be reversed or reformed. Usually the good wine was given first. And later, after the taste buds had been sufficiently intoxicated, the poorer quality wine was served. The master of ceremonies noted, completely unaware of anything out of the ordinary, that the miracle that had been wrought by Jesus reversed proprietary customs. Again, the reversal of norms is significant.

Somewhere along the line Jesus decided that the wedding provided an opportune circumstance for the public announcement or display of His divinity. This was the first of several such announcements to be made by the fact of miracles. Water became wine. What was ordinary (water) became extraordinary (fine wine). What was used for ritual purification (water) became a sign of covenantal consummation (wine).[6] Hardly anyone was even aware of Jesus' involvement.

The interplay between the human and divine realms regarding this miracle simply indicated that ordinary events, in this case a wedding, could be used to reveal God's hand in human history. The miracle simply pointed to the presence of God (Jesus Christ) in the midst of a covenantal (marriage) celebration. The covenant Lord was

---

6 According to Jewish religious law, Shabbat is observed from just before sunset on Friday evening until the appearance of three stars in the sky on Saturday night. Shabbat is ushered in by lighting candles and reciting a blessing.

at hand. The story was that Jesus had done it. So, it set the standard that all of the signs of divine presence or miracles would point to Him. This first miracle served as an unrecognized announcement to the world: Emmanuel! (which means: God with us).

There is no natural explanation suggested for this miracle. Water becomes wine, the ordinary become extraordinary, and the natural order of social norms was reversed by the presence of Jesus. And so we can ask: what really was the miracle at Cana? Was it the water changing into wine? Or the ordinary becoming extraordinary? Or was it the reversal of covenantal patterns? To what does this miracle point?

THE WOMAN AT THE WELL

Secret Food

"Just then his disciples came back. They marveled that he was talking with a woman, but no one said, 'What do you seek?' or, 'Why are you talking with her?' So the woman left her water jar and went away into town and said to the people, 'Come, see a man who told me all that I ever did. Can this be the Christ?' They went out of the town and were coming to him. Meanwhile the disciples were urging him, saying, 'Rabbi, eat.' But he said to them, 'I have food to eat that you do not know about.' So the disciples said to one another, 'Has anyone brought him something to eat?' Jesus said to them, 'My food is to do the will of him who sent me and to accomplish his work. Do you not say, "There are yet four months, then comes the harvest"? Look, I tell you, lift up your eyes, and see that the fields are white for harvest. Already the one who reaps is receiving wages and gathering fruit for eternal life, so that sower and reaper may rejoice together. For here the saying holds true, 'One sows and another reaps.' I sent you to reap that for which you did not labor. Others have labored, and you have entered into their labor." —John 4:27-38

As soon as Jesus told the woman that He was the Messiah, the disciples returned with the groceries. Their entrance into Jesus' conversation with the woman ended it. As soon as they arrived, she left. That shouldn't be surprising. She was outnumbered, the only woman among men, and the only Samaritan among Jews. So she left.

Overwhelmed by the power of the Holy Spirit through her encounter with Jesus, she left in such a flurry that she forgot her water pot. Imagine being in the presence of Jesus, face to face with the Messiah. It would be one thing if you didn't know that He was Messiah, but if you knew, it would be awesome! You'd probably forget your water pot, too.

When the disciples returned they immediately wondered about His involvement with this woman. No doubt, they treated Jesus as Lord and Master when they returned, deferring to Him and engaging Him in conversation that suggested that they believed Him to be the Messiah, as He had suggested to her. She may have noticed their deference, and had second thoughts about who she had been talking to.

They marveled that He had been talking with a woman. We don't know what their marveling meant. It could have been a kind of gawking because Jesus openly violated Jewish custom by talking with a Samaritan—and a woman at that! Imagine their offense because His relationship with the woman could cause trouble with the local elders. They may have thought it was dangerous and foolish on His part. Besides, they also held the Samaritans in disrespect.

Or they may have thought it was marvelous that Jesus, the Lord and Master of the Universe, would be so considerate as to take time for a Samaritan—and a woman at that! They may have thought that His talking with her was a good and wonderful thing. It was just like Jesus to want to bring salvation to all His people, and not to overlook even the least. They had different opinions about most things. This situation would have been no different in that regard. So, we can only conclude that they held differing opinions.

Yet, not one of them said anything to Him about it. The passage is written to suggest that the disciples were thinking questions like, "What do You want from this woman?" or "Why are you talking with her?" But John makes it a point to note that not one of them *said* anything about it. More than likely, as the disciples came into the picture they began talking with Jesus and simply ignored the woman, who subsequently left as it occurred to her that all of these men seriously regarded Jesus as the Messiah.

Maybe Jesus intended His disciples to see Him talking with a Samaritan and to conclude from it that the separation between Jews and Samaritans was supposed to end. That was precisely the revelation that Peter received from his dream when heaven opened and a great sheet of clean and unclean beasts came down (Acts 10:11-15). The Holy Spirit directed Peter to eat everything—clean and unclean, thus confirming this same idea that the divisions between people and foods was at an end. All foods were clean, all religious distinctions were subservient to Christ.

Jesus was also breaking down the patterns of discrimination between men and women. He consistently taught and addressed Himself to women in a manner that suggested and promoted their full personhood. Likely, Jesus meant to do both of these things. It was consistent with His teaching of universal emancipation, what Paul called freedom in Christ (Galatians 5:1). This is only to say that Jesus treated people as if they were each important.

The Elders

The woman, having returned to Sychar, spoke first with the men at the gate of the city, because that was where the men gathered and she could not avoid them as she entered the town. Generally, women would have been found further into the city, engaged in daily chores, at home, tending the children and households. She spoke to the men because they were responsible for the oversight of the city. She told the authorities about meeting Jesus. It is unlikely that she reported Him simply because He, a Jew, had spoken to her, a Samaritan. Her interest was not to prosecute Him. Although the town elders might have gone out to Him with that in mind.

Rather, she told them how He had known all about the sins of her life. Her words, "Come, see a Man who told me all things that I ever did" (v. 29), were an exaggeration of the truth. Jesus didn't tell her literally everything that she had ever done. Rather, He identified her major sins, and that is the sense in which she spoke. He knew all about her in the sense of knowing all her "dirt." He knew things that she knew He shouldn't have known.

The woman was a liar. Jesus had caught her teasing a lie about her five husbands. Her sins hadn't come to an end just because she met Jesus. When Jesus exposed her lie, she didn't stop lying. Exaggeration is the habit of liars, and that is just what she did. She exaggerated, even though she probably didn't mean to. After a while, it just becomes a habit. She exaggerated. He "told me all things that I ever did," she said. That is, all the things she didn't want anyone to know. The sins that need to be forgiven are the very things that sinners don't want God to know about because they are afraid that He will not forgive them. And they sure don't want anyone else to know about them, either! But Jesus knew them anyway. When will people learn that you can't hide sins from God?

On the trip back to the city the woman went from being an unrepentant sinner to becoming a missionary. It's a common path. The woman had found Christ, and having found Him, she wanted others to share in her discovery, perhaps to prove or test it. Evangelism is one of the fruits of salvation. Where there is no evangelism, salvation can be doubted. But her motivation was simple and sincere. She called the men at the gate to come and see Christ for themselves.

The way the question is phrased in the New King James Version (NKJV) suggests, albeit weakly, that the woman was not sure that Jesus was the Christ. It reads, "Could this be the Christ?" (v. 29). But the King James Version (KJV) translates the verse, "is not this the Christ?" The first reading gives a stronger sense of the doubt, but the KJV translation puts a statement in the woman's mouth that challenged the men to refute it. She may have doubted, but her doubt was subsidiary to her hope.

How could the woman have been sure? Faith is not knowledge. Faith is the assurance of things not seen. She did the intelligent thing. She sought the counsel of others. She went to the city elders asking them to confirm or deny her initial thought that Jesus may be the Messiah.

Any elder worth his salt would not have believed the woman at this point. She did not have a trustworthy reputation in town. Surely, her sins were known by others. But the simple faith and heartfelt response of the woman was sufficient to convince the elders that they needed to check out her story. So, they went to see Jesus, to evaluate the situation for themselves.

The Disciples

In the meantime Jesus' disciples had returned with food and encouraged Him to eat. Jesus' answer in verse 32, "I have food to eat of which you do not know," is John's rendition of Matthew 4:4, "Man shall not live by bread alone, but by every word that proceeds out of the mouth of God." More important than food for the body is food for the soul. Jesus also said in Matthew 10:28,

> "do not fear those who kill the body, but are not able to kill the soul. But rather fear Him who can destroy both soul and body in hell."

His point was that the soul is more important than the body.

But Jesus was not forsaking food for the gospel, as if ministry were more important than eating. Ordinary bodily needs and functions cannot and should not be avoided. He was not modeling or calling His people to ignore their bodily needs for the sake of ministry. Ministry is not such a high calling that it should override bodily functions. Not at all! Jesus was simply modeling and calling His people to do first what first needs to be done. He was laying out gospel priorities, not justifying people who are so otherworldly that they are no earthly good. Jesus calls His people to manifest the Holy Spirit in the world, but simultaneously to not be so much a part of the world as to be just like the world. Jesus did not pray for God to take His disciples out of the world, but that God would keep them from evil (John 17:15). Christians must live in the midst of evil, there is no other option. But we are not to compromise with it.

Nonetheless, the disciples, poor oafs that they were, misunderstood what Jesus meant (v. 33). And because they missed it, we, as the readers of John's gospel, can mock them for their ignorance. By noting that they *missed* it, we are able to *get* it. They seemed to think that Jesus was talking about meat and potatoes. John's emphasis of the fact that the disciples misunderstood Jesus, makes those who actually understand Jesus to be the real recipients of His grace in this story. If they missed it, Jesus wasn't talking to them. The Lord speaks to those who understand, for those who have ears to hear.[1]

The literary genius of the Gospel of John opens an opportunity for you and me to hear Jesus and receive the Holy Spirit through

---

[1] See Deuteronomy 29:4; Ezekiel 12:2; Matthew 11:15 13:9,43; Mark 4:9,23 7:16; Luke 8:8; 14:35.

Scripture. Because they missed it, Jesus went on to explain it to them. But this word *them* points to a different *them* than the *them* in verse 32. In verse 32 Jesus spoke to the disciples who encouraged Him to eat some of the food they had purchased. As that conversation developed, the men from Sychar, to whom the woman had gone to tell of Jesus, had arrived to check Jesus out for themselves. It makes sense that the men of Sychar gathered with the disciples as Jesus preached verses 34-38. These verses provide a major teaching and they converted many Samaritans.

Jesus told them that the accomplishment of God's will nourishes the soul. It was true for Jesus, and its true for those who follow Him. However, Jesus spoke not only of God's will, but of God's work as well. We know that God's work in and through Jesus abounds, for He has accomplished the salvation of the gentiles by His atoning sacrifice on the cross. That is God's work. That's what He did, not something that we do—nor need we do it, for He has accomplished it already. But at this point in the story, Christ's atoning work on the cross had not yet been accomplished.

So, what is God's will suggested in v. 34? That indeed is the question and the rub. It is not a question that I can answer for you, or you for me. It is a question that each individual must take to the Scriptures to study for him- or herself. Each of us must take this question to the Lord in prayer. Because faith is like a journey, God's direction must be continuously sought and heeded, lest the journey drift from God's course, God's intended destination. Prayer and Bible study are the primary tools for discerning God's will. All disciples must engage them on a regular basis.

The Work

Jesus said that doing God's will and work nourished Him. Jesus didn't do God's will and work because He enjoyed it, though He did. He was crucified because of it! Nonetheless, He did it because it was life to Him, and brought Him great joy in spite of the difficulties. God's will and work are as important as food. God's people are fed by their service to Him. For the faithful, service to God is not an option. It *must* be done, freely done of their own accord. Disciples don't have a choice in the matter because disciples do what the master wants them to do.

Jesus then referred to a common saying among the people, that there were four months between planting and harvest. He contrasted the common saying with the teaching that He brought. In essence, He said that there was normally a period of time between seed and harvest, but that with regard to spiritual matters the seed that had been planted in the Samaritan woman had already produced fruit and that there was, among the men of Sychar who had joined them, a harvest to be reaped. When the harvest is ready, arguments must be put aside and the work of the harvest engaged, lest the fruit spoil on the vine.

By speaking of farming Jesus was able to communicate a spiritual truth in terms that were familiar to them. Farmers paid a great deal of attention to the seasons and crops, but here Jesus pointed out how little attention they paid to spiritual concerns. A spiritual harvest was upon them, and they were unprepared.

They knew that harvest of the fields always requires immediate attention. When crops are ripe, they have to be gathered immediately. Consequently, the reapers' wage was very high in order to insure ample workers. Delays could not be recouped. What was lost was lost, so the farmers and their workers made harvest a top priority.

This was precisely Jesus' message. The spiritual harvest that was upon them required immediate attention. He told them that not only did reapers receive excellent wages to meet of the needs of temporal life, but they would also store up fruit for eternal life. In the glories of eternal life, those who reap can rejoice with those who have sown, even those who sowed spiritual seed lifetimes earlier.

Jesus immediately turned to explain this issue of how sowers and reapers can rejoice together by contrasting the wisdom of God with the wisdom of the world. In farming, those who sowed did not necessarily see the fruit of their work. "One sows and another reaps" (v. 37) was the established wisdom. But in the eternity of heaven, Jesus said, sowers and reapers rejoice together, but only after the work of reaping has been completed.

Jesus also noted that the spiritual harvest before them had been sown by others. Likely, He meant the biblical prophets of antiquity. Surely, He didn't mean current prophets because Samaria had fallen into apostasy. And He didn't mean Himself because earlier He noted that the woman had already known of the prophecy of Messiah and eagerly expected Him (v. 25). The seed of her expectation had been sown many, many years earlier. Jesus simply built upon the seed of her Messianic expectation.

As Jesus fulfilled that prophecy, the expectation of the people came to a head and produced an immediate spiritual harvest. It was in this sense that Jesus told His disciples that they had entered into the labors of others (v. 38). There was no time to argue about who would get the credit for planting the gospel seed. It didn't matter.

Two things were taught by Jesus here. First, the Kingdom of God was a cooperative effort. Many people would be involved, building upon the work of one another, even if they didn't recognize one another. Secondly, the Kingdom was on a strict timetable, in the same way that farming was on a timetable. When it was harvest time, everything else took a back seat.

No Honor

Many Samaritans from that town believed in him because of the woman's testimony, 'He told me all that I ever did.' So when the Samaritans came to him, they asked him to stay with them, and he stayed there two days. And many more believed because of his word. They said to the woman, 'It is no longer because of what you said that we believe, for we have heard for ourselves, and we know that this is indeed the Savior of the world.' After the two days he departed for Galilee. (For Jesus himself had testified that a prophet has no honor in his own hometown.) So when he came to Galilee, the Galileans welcomed him, having seen all that he had done in Jerusalem at the feast. For they too had gone to the feast. —John 4:39-45

It would be interesting to know exactly how many people believed because of the testimony of the Samaritan woman. But all Scripture says is that "many of the Samaritans of that city believed" (v. 39). Indeed, believing is the central miracle of this story.

The Samaritan woman had become a new believer. Yet, she had barely begun to believe the gospel herself. She shared what belief she had, and because of her willingness to share what she knew, what she believed, others believed. Again, it is doubtful that they came to an instantaneous, full-blown, orthodox Christian understanding of the gospel because of the testimony of this woman. But she shared in a simple, straight forward manner, and the Lord used it.

We should take notice that the Lord uses the heart-felt praises of His people to work His will. It is not necessary that everyone who shares a belief or a testimony needs to have it spit-polished to a brilliant shine before sharing it with others. What is most important in our sharing is that we share honestly, that we say what we know, and admit what we don't know. There are two aspects of sharing our faith honestly that deserve mention.

The Witness

First, we should speak what we know plainly and simply, without embellishment. Too often people want to be seen as highly spiritual and intelligent people, so they tailor their witness to conform to the image they have of themselves. They want to show off their new spirituality. But witnesses should stick to the facts of the case and, if anything, under embellish rather than exaggerate. By keeping their witness plain and simple, they will encourage their hearers to ask questions and enter into discussion for clarification—and thereby communicate even more effectively.

Second, Christians should readily admit what they do not know. People too often think that they need to know everything before they can share their faith. "What if someone asks me a question that I don't know?" people fear. The correct answer is always the plain truth. By saying, "I don't know," we keep from embellishing or exaggerating—or just making something up that sounds good. A simple "I don't know" will preserve the integrity of the truth. But it also lets others know that its alright not to know everything. If Christians have to know everything about the Bible and theology before they share their faith with someone, there will be few professing Christians indeed!

The Samaritan woman shared her experience of Jesus. The experience of believers varies considerably, so witnesses need not over emphasize *their* particular experience. Rather, the witness should highlight *Jesus*. Christians should always keep their eyes on Jesus, and especially when they are witnessing. As soon as Christians begin to compare and contrast their own various faith experiences, confusion breaks out because there is a great variety of religious experience.

The personal experience of believers need not be denied, only kept in proper perspective. The sharing of personal experience should always point to Christ. Too often people share in such a way that Christ is made to serve the interests of *their* particular experience. When that happens, people begin to expect that all Christians must have similar kinds of experiences. The better way is to testify to Christ rather than to one's own personal experience of Christ. The difference may be subtle, but it is important.

THE INVITATION

Having heard Jesus (vs. 34-38), the Samaritans of Sychar were so impressed that they invited Him to stay with them. They liked what they heard, and wanted more. Jesus was able to spend two days with them.

It would be glorious to know all that Jesus taught and said in those two days, but this is one of many places where Scripture is silent. Yet, the silence of Scripture does not fail to instruct. The silence of Scripture provides space for meditation and reflection—and room for the Holy Spirit to do His work. An effective witness knows when to speak and how to speak so that people will hear what is said. But he also knows when not to speak. He knows when saying too much is worse than saying nothing at all.

The Samaritans invited Jesus to stay with them. *They* invited Him. There are at least two lessons to learn from this fact. First, if Jesus is not part of your life, it is only because *you* have not invited Him. The Samaritans, unlike the Jews, wanted Jesus' instruction. Their hearts were open to the Lord, in contrast to the Jews, who believed that they already knew all they needed to know about God. Their hearts were closed. Second, Jesus didn't force Himself upon them. He knew that people must be willing to hear Him, and when they aren't, His evangelists must shake the dust from their feet and move on (Matthew 10:14).

Again, notice that the evangelist did not invite those whom he was evangelizing to receive Jesus. Rather, those who were being evangelized did the inviting. The real invitation is not to invite people to receive Jesus, because they can't receive Jesus until they are ready. But once they are ready, they will do the inviting themselves. That's an important point because a premature invitation is worse than powerless because it can actually push people away from the Lord.

After two days with Jesus the Samaritan men gave their own testimonies, where before they had believed because the woman had shared her testimony with them. That in itself is odd because she was not a trustworthy woman. But perhaps they saw something different about her following her contact with Jesus. At any rate, now they "believed because of His own word" (v. 41). They had seen His faith, and heard His Word, acknowledging that it is the faith and word of Jesus that is the critical element of belief.

It is not *my* faith or *your* faith that saves, it is *Christ's* faith that saves. The Holy Spirit gives us *His* faith, which is much stronger than *our* faith. We must make it our own, of course—or rather, we must be made His own by it. The woman did not insist that they experience Jesus as she had. Her testimony simply pointed them to Jesus. She was not the subject of her testimony, Christ was. The fact that this process of evangelism was then reproduced in Sychar is evidenced by the fact that John tells us that "many more" had come to belief in those two days. The men of Sychar then shared their testimony as the woman had—by simply pointing others to Christ.

The Confession

Jesus was received and proclaimed to be "the Christ, the Savior of the World," by Samaritans at Sychar. Remember that the Samaritans were half-breeds in the eyes of Israel. They were scorned because they had broken the Covenant.[2] Jerusalem Jews considered them to be apostate half-Jews—worse than non-Jews because they had turned their backs on God. Yet these Samaritans now received Jesus and believed.

---

2 "Samaritans believe that their worship, which is based on the Samaritan Pentateuch, is the true religion of the ancient Israelites from before the Babylonian captivity, preserved by those who remained in the Land of Israel, as opposed to Judaism, which they see as a related but altered and amended religion, brought back by those returning from the Babylonian Captivity. The Samaritans believe that Mount Gerizim was the original Holy Place of Israel from the time that Joshua conquered Canaan. The major issue between Jews and Samaritans has always been the location of the Chosen Place to worship God: The Temple Mount of Moriah in Jerusalem according to the Jewish faith or Mount Gerizim according to the Samaritan faith." Source: wiki2.org/en/Samaritans

Why would Samaritans be more open to Jesus than the Jews, particularly the leaders of the Second Temple Jewish establishment? The answer is quite simple: the Samaritans had a sense that they were sinners and in need of salvation. But the Jerusalem Jews, and particularly the established religious leaders did not believe themselves to be sinners. They thought that they were already upholding God's law and, therefore, were not sinners. And thus, not in need of salvation.

Sin is always the key to receiving Jesus. When people do not believe themselves to be sinners, they perceive no need for Jesus. The modern secular world has done everything it can to eradicate sin from modern awareness. Secular psychologists and educators insist that sin is outdated, that the doctrine of the Fall overly emphasizes the negative, to the detriment of personal self-esteem. They tell us that people need more self-esteem and less attention to their sins, errors, and mistakes. They tell us that people will become more kind and loving if they receive more positive support for their self-esteem, and less accusation for their sins.

But this modern, secular theory runs directly counter to the teaching and testimony of Scripture. Scripture shows us that the confession of personal sinfulness is a prerequisite for acknowledging God's grace in Christ. The old time preachers emphasized human sin and reaped great harvests of souls for Christ. In contrast, the authorities of our day keep people away from Christ by convincing them that they are not sinners. The contemporary worldview keeps people away from Scripture, and away from the time-tested, God-approved methods of finding salvation in Christ by ridiculing such methods as being unsophisticated relics of a past that are not worth remembering.

And they do it by the mere suggestion that people are not sinners. Unfortunately, people are very eager to believe this lie. Of course, people want to hear that they are not sinners, that they are basically good, that God's *a priori* condemnation of them is unfair. So, they flock to hear such erroneous teaching. But

> "There is a way which seems right to man, but the end of it is the way of death" (Proverbs 14:12).

Only sinners need Christ. Christ has come to cure sin. God set up a dynamic tension in the human heart that must be resolved. That tension pulls between sin and salvation. Sin and salvation, as differing doctrines and competing lifestyles, cannot coexist. One must overcome the other.

Jesus Christ provides salvation, which Scripture predicts will ultimately overcome all sin. The world, pulling in the opposite direction, offers sin—sanitized, pasteurized, and authorized—as salvation from God's backwardness! The world does all it can to belittle Scripture. It used to be that God's salvation openly warred against worldly sin. That war still rages, but the modern world has devised a way to promote its sinfulness without directly engaging the issue of God's salvation by appealing to self-esteem, by convincing people that they are not sinners. The ruse is that talk about sin is out of style, and no longer appropriate in a modern, enlightened world. The lie is that the world has moved beyond the primitive need for such a thing.

People like believing themselves not to be sinners. It makes people comfortable. It makes it easy to ignore the issue of salvation. By ignoring the call and demands of salvation, people can deny the tension between sin and salvation. The easing of that tension then produces a feeling of relative relaxation, of peace.

But because the tension has been denied and not overcome, the feeling of relaxation or peace is only a shallow, temporary experience. The same kind of thing happened in Jeremiah's day. He called it a false peace, a shallow peace that could not heal (Jeremiah 6-8). The short-run prognosis of this post-modern situation is the wholesale embrace of the teaching and methods of self-esteem, the continuing denial of sin, and escalating hostility toward the practice of biblical Christianity. In the past this kind of trend has led to social disasters of one kind or another.

This is likely the same hostility that Jesus encountered from the Jewish establishment in His day. They believed that they held the only keys to salvation, and Jesus threatened that belief and the religious establishment that rested upon it. Consequently, the religious authorities opposed Jesus zealously.

But the Samaritans opened their arms to Him. They received Him and believed the gospel at the outset of His ministry. Surely the belief of the Samaritans fanned the flames of the opposition to Jesus by the Jewish establishment. As the ministry of Jesus unfolded, there was much opposition generated by the Pharisees and Sadducees. But time and again Samaritans and other social outcasts came to faith because they were convicted of their own sin.

The Problem

The point is that the grace of salvation produces the conviction of sin. If a person believes himself to be not guilty, he does not need mercy. This is the reason that people do not respond to Jesus today. When the gospel is preached and people are not brought to the Lord, it is likely that one of two problems are present.

Either preachers have not laid the proper foundation for the gospel—that foundation being the doctrine of total depravity or sin in conjunction with the grace and mercy of God. No one else in society is able lay such a foundation. Scripture alone testifies to it. Consequently, it is the sole responsibility of gospel preaching. The vast majority of people will not seek a physician unless they perceive themselves to be sick.

Or the other problem is that people, being convinced of the truth of the secular perspective, doubt and disagree and don't understand God and the Bible. Because they dislike the doctrine of sin, they complain and resist and do everything they can to undermine the effort to lay the gospel foundation of sin and depravity. And, again, such people think that they have no need of God's grace, mercy, or salvation.

People can sometimes tolerate the sinfulness of humanity in general, but when their own personal sins are brought into the picture—particularly in public, the proverbial *fit* hits the *shan*. It is an embarrassment to have to repent of particular sins in public. People would rather continue to sin than to submit to such personal embarrassment. Their self-esteem crowds out the humility necessary for repentance. And therein lies the rub.

Jesus said, "Blessed are they that mourn! For they shall be comforted" (Matthew 5:4). Blessed are those who repent of their sins, publicly or privately—it matters little, for theirs is the comfort of salvation. To a humble sinner, it doesn't matter if their confession is private or public because it is an acknowledgment of God's truth. And God's truth is more important than their embarrassment.

The Official's Son

Healing Miracle

"After the two days he departed for Galilee. (For Jesus himself had testified that a prophet has no honor in his own hometown.) So when he came to Galilee, the Galileans welcomed him, having seen all that he had done in Jerusalem at the feast. For they too had gone to the feast. So he came again to Cana in Galilee, where he had made the water wine. And at Capernaum there was an official whose son was ill. When this man heard that Jesus had come from Judea to Galilee, he went to him and asked him to come down and heal his son, for he was at the point of death. So Jesus said to him, 'Unless you see signs and wonders you will not believe.' The official said to him, 'Sir, come down before my child dies.' Jesus said to him, 'Go; your son will live.' The man believed the word that Jesus spoke to him and went on his way. As he was going down, his servants met him and told him that his son was recovering. So he asked them the hour when he began to get better, and they said to him, 'Yesterday at the seventh hour the fever left him.' The father knew that was the hour when Jesus had said to him, 'Your son will live.' And he himself believed, and all his household. This was now the second sign that Jesus did when he had come from Judea to Galilee." —John 4:43-54

Jesus left Sychar and went to Galilee. Verse 44 comments upon verse 43, as if to explain why Jesus went to Galilee, "a prophet has no honor in his own country." But it raises as many questions as it answers. One of the questions being, what is the country of Jesus?

First and foremost Jesus was a Jew, which would make Judah His country. Born in Bethlehem, only a few miles from Jerusalem, the capital city of Judah, Jesus was surely a Jew. But how far did the Jewish nation extend? In Jesus' day it did not include Samaria, the area just north of Judah. Perhaps in the eyes of Rome Judah included Samaria, but not in the eyes of Jerusalem Jews.

Samaria then stood between Judah and Galilee. Yet, Nazareth was in Galilee, and Jesus was also known as the Man of Nazareth (Luke 24:19). Jesus grew up in Nazareth, and had many friends and relatives there. So Galilee could be considered His country as well. But, legally (for tax purposes) He was born in Bethlehem, and that made Him a Jew. Besides, we know that Jesus had no honor among the Jerusalem Jews, particularly among the Jewish establishment. The reference to a prophet's lack of honor among his own people had been most likely directed at Jerusalem, where His reception had been cold.

The usual explanation of this proverbial saying about a prophet's honor among family is that friends and relatives will not honor someone they knew in diapers. People think that they know the character of a child, and don't allow for growth and maturity—much less the change of values that come with regeneration.

Home

But when we realize that Jesus was raised in Nazareth, we find that this explanation breaks down. His friends and family in Nazareth should have been the ones who granted Jesus no honor because they had known Him as a young boy. But that is not the case. Another explanation must be sought.

In the biblical tradition all prophets were Jewish, and all prophecies centered upon the Jewish nation. Foreigners and heathen nations were often used by God to affect the Jews. Nonetheless, the Jewish establishment never honored their prophets. Prophets were always calling the establishment to task for straying from God's way.

For these reasons I think that the "his" of verse 44 may refer to Jesus, rather than to a generic prophet. But even if the original saying referred to a generic prophet, Jesus may have used it in reference to Himself to make the point about Jerusalem.

We must remember that His use of the saying occurred at Sychar, where Jesus had spent two days teaching because of the testimony of the woman at the well. One of the issues for the woman at the well had been the tension and division between the Jews and the Samaritans (John 4:20).

While the woman had raised the issue as a deflection to try to move Jesus away from a consideration of her personal sins, it remained a prominent issue in the minds of Jews and Samaritans. Perhaps her concern was related to something that Jesus taught during those two days. We can understand the Samaritans to have believed that Jesus had sided with them in this matter because He said that prophets never fared well in Judah. He may have been trying to explain why He was ministering in Samaria, and to elicit sympathy and support for His ministry there.

At any rate Jesus went from Samaria to Galilee. And like the Samaritans, the Galileans also received Jesus. John said that they had received Him because of what He had done at the feast. That would have been the recent Passover feast in Jerusalem, where Jesus had driven the Jewish money changers out of the Temple and predicted that the Temple would be destroyed and rebuilt (John 2:14-15). We know that Temple worship had been an issue for the woman at the well, and for the Samaritans in general (John 4:45). John 2:23 also noted that many believed as a result of Jesus' Temple activity that day.

If this scenario is correct, Jesus would have been understood by both Jews and Samaritans to have more affinity with the Samaritans than with the Jews because the Jewish establishment opposed Him, and His Samaritan support may have also been a major source of His conflict with Jewish authorities. Remember that Jesus had aimed His ministry at the lost sheep of Israel (Matthew 10:6) Jesus targeted first those who knew they were lost—Samaritans and other Jews of the dispersion, and second, those caught in the rotting structures of Second Temple Judaism.

In verses 43-45, Jesus entered into Cana of Galilee, where sometime earlier He had attended a wedding. Only friends and family attend weddings, which means that Jesus was no stranger in Galilee. Word of Jesus' exploits in Jerusalem had preceded His arrival in Galilee. His audience was growing.

Disconnect

At the wedding He had performed a miracle, but cautioned His mother and disciples that the ensuing miracle had nothing to do with His ministry. His hour had not yet come. It was as if He consented to perform the miracle in order to state that the miracle had nothing to do with the gospel He preached. This was a major theme of Jesus.[1]

It was the first miracle Jesus performed and it got the disciples attention—so much so that "His disciples believed in Him" (John 2:11). It was done for their sake, but should not be confused with the gospel. Jesus said that it had nothing to do with His mission (John 2:4). Yet, He performed it for the sake of His disciples, perhaps to draw them deeper into their fledgling faith, and probably in order to attract more people to His ministry and mission.

It was of this event, and Jesus' understanding of it, that John reminded his readers in verse 46. At the outset of the healing of the nobleman's son, Jesus emphasized this understanding of the relationship between miracles and gospel. His curt statement in verse 48 carries a sense of righteous indignation regarding the popular desire for signs and miracles.

> "Unless you see signs and wonders you will not believe." (John 4:48).

The nobleman was neither a Jew nor a Samaritan. He was a foreigner, a Gentile. In that regard he was an unbiased observer, not tainted by the enmity between the Jews and the Samaritans. He wasn't caught up in that history. Yet, he sought healing for his son.

The Samaritans had been Covenant breakers. The Jews were rotting in the administrative entanglements of their man-made traditions. And the Gentiles had no source of healing. The whole world was lost! Jesus had come for those who would be saved, wherever He could find them—Jew, Samaritan, or Gentile.

---

1 *Marking God's Word—Understanding Jesus*, Phillip A. Ross, Pilgrim Platform, Marietta, Ohio, 2006.

Jesus clearly scolded the nobleman, and by implication all who seek miracles more than they seek the Kingdom of God. Again, Jesus took the opportunity to teach that wonders and miracles are not the gospel. He didn't deny that wonders and miracles exist. Clearly they were real; He manifested them Himself. But they were not the gospel!

Initially, the nobleman had no interest in the gospel. He just wanted his son healed. So it is with too many people; they want miraculous healing, but don't care about what Jesus taught. This story is about the general failure of most people to connect healing and salvation with doctrine. Salvation comes from hearing and receiving the gospel, and produces adherence to God's righteousness. Salvation is not a miraculous touch from a magic wand that guarantees life without tears in some nether world. No, salvation issues from grace through faith, and the eternal life that flows from the righteousness of God, on earth as it is in heaven.

The nobleman had no concern for Christ's doctrine—until his son was saved. When he made the connection between Jesus' words and his son's salvation, then he himself believed. When he opened himself up to hear and receive the doctrine of Christ, then he believed.

The fruit of his belief was the same as the faithful fruit of the woman at the well, and of the men of Sychar. They had evangelized their families and friends. Faith is contagious. It produces gospel fruit. Not only did the nobleman believe, but his whole household believed as well. He also shared his faith with his family. Don't overlook the importance of family-centered evangelism.

Signs & Wonders

The Jews were so caught up in the Messianic predictions of the age that they sought signs and wonders more than truth (John 2:18, 1 Corinthians 1:22). And yet, it was not just the Jews alone. Here we see that Samaritans, Galileans, and Gentiles were all infected with the confusion between signs (miracles) and gospel (doctrine). People flocked to see signs and wonders, but few stayed for the heart of the gospel (John 6:66). John reminded his readers again that this was the second sign Jesus did—the second time He had cautioned people about the relationship between miracles and gospel.

We are still (or perhaps *again* in our day) in the grip of this confusion. Our confusion has new names and new theories, but the character of Postmodern belief is the same as this ancient error. There is an apocalyptic fervor burning in our day that has the same earmarks as the Messianism that clouded the judgment of people in Jesus' day.

People seek signs and wonders and miraculous healings, but ignore the gospel of Christ. People sing and dance, shout and praise the Lord, but many fail to live Christian lives. Polls indicate that there is little or no difference between the lifestyles and morality of those who profess Christianity and those who don't.

Modern Evangelicalism has thrown open its arms to the world. And by doing so it has embraced various unbiblical teachings, practices, and techniques. There is little difference between the educational techniques of Sunday School and the secular classroom. What I mean is not that secular education uses biblical content or techniques, but rather, Christians employ much of the content and techniques of secular education, i.e., age segmented education. The church pays too much lip service to God, but too often follows the ways of the world.

The healing of our nation will require the return, not just to biblical values, but to biblical methods of education as well. Such a return can only begin in the church. For too long the church has followed every new wind of educational reform coming down the pike. The church must stop following the ways of the world, and begin leading with the ways of God. Contrary to popular opinion the healing of America will involve more doctrine than miracle, more gospel than political reorganization, more ordinary repentance than pastoral charisma.

THE POOL OF BETHESDA

WILT THOU?

"After this there was a feast of the Jews, and Jesus went up to Jerusalem. Now there is in Jerusalem by the Sheep Gate a pool, in Aramaic called Bethesda, which has five roofed colonnades. In these lay a multitude of invalids—blind, lame, and paralyzed [waiting for the moving of the water;] [for an angel of the Lord went down at certain seasons into the pool, and stirred the water: whoever stepped in first after the stirring of the water was healed of whatever disease he had.] One man was there who had been an invalid for thirty-eight years. When Jesus saw him lying there and knew that he had already been there a long time, he said to him, 'Do you want to be healed?' The sick man answered him, 'Sir, I have no one to put me into the pool when the water is stirred up, and while I am going another steps down before me.' Jesus said to him, 'Get up, take up your bed, and walk.'
—John 5:1-8

Twice now John has made a point of telling his readers that Jesus taught that miraculous healing was not the gospel—both times in Cana of Galilee, once at the wedding and again with the healing of the nobleman's son. That theme continues into chapter five with the story of the healing of the man at the Pool of Bethesda.

The purpose of the Bethesda story is to reveal the grip that the power of superstition had upon God's people, and to show how to escape from it. The purpose of Jesus' ministry was to break the hold that religious superstition—even Jewish Temple superstition—had upon the poor and infirm, to set them free to follow God. As usual, the establishment profited from the foolishness of God's people. Jesus tended to minister among the lowest classes of people—not exclusively, but generally—for a variety of reasons.

To begin this analysis, we must first locate the Pool of Bethesda. It's location is important, and would have been common knowledge among people at the time, so mention of it would have been unnecessary because it was assumed to be common knowledge among those to whom Jesus spoke. But it is not known to us today.

Bethesda means "house of mercy." John made a point of identifying the word in Hebrew. *Bethesda* is a compound of two words. The first is *bayith* (בַּיִת), which is most often translated as house, but also as *temple, prison,* and even, *dungeon*. These latter translations are significant because the Pool of Bethesda was located near the sheep gate, "between the tower of Meah and the chamber of the corner, or gate of the guard house or prison gate."[1]

The second Hebrew word which makes *Bethesda* is *checed* (חֶסֶד), which is most often translated as *mercy, kindness,* and *goodness,* but also pity, or reproach. An act of mercy can also be an act taken in pity. The house of mercy could also be a house of pity.

THE POOL

The Bethesda pool was a reservoir of water that attracted people. Over time five porches had been built around this reservoir for protection from the hot desert sun. Because of the location near the Roman prison it is unlikely that it was originally built as a swimming or bathing pool. More likely it was originally related to the drainage system of the Temple. There has been speculation that the pool of Bethesda had been fed in part by water that had been used to either wash the sacrifices and/or the altar after sacrifice.[2] That water then fed into the Bethesda pool giving it what the people believed were "spiritual" qualities. How so?

---

1 *Home Bible Study Dictionary*, A. R. Fausset, Kregel Publications, Grand Rapids, Michigan, reprinted 1987.
2 Hammond, referred to by J. C. Ryle in *John*, Volume 1, The Banner of Truth Trust, Carlisle, PA, 1869, reprint 1987,

The Pool of Bethesda was related to the Temple drainage system, which terminated outside the city wall, near the prison. As the water flowed from the Temple to the pool it would have "stirred" the water in the pool. The water of the Bethesda pool was superstitiously perceived to have healing powers probably because of its association with Temple use. The water had been used for cleansing and sacrificial rites in the Temple and was probably thought to have a lingering spiritual power of some kind.

The Bethesda pool was in an out of the way location in Jerusalem, as you would expect a drainage system location to have. In addition, it was not the custom for the Jewish establishment to highlight or even allow the blind, lame, and paralyzed in a prominent part of the city. According to Hammond, Bethesda, near the sheep gate or prison, was outside the city walls, near a poor part of the city. Because Jesus often ministered with the poor, ill, and infirm, the setting of this miracle is certainly in keeping with the tenor of Jesus' ministry.

The Superstition

According to John's account, an angel stirred up the water and the first person who got in the water after the stirring would be healed. This was probably a simple restatement of the common, superstitious understanding of how the miracle of Bethesda was supposed to have worked. This was what people believed. John was not saying that this was what actually happened, but that this was what people believed. This was the superstition.

Modern scholarship supports this view. *Word Biblical Commentary*[3] indicates that verse 4, "may reflect an old tradition, it formed no part of the text of the Gospel."[4] Beasley-Murray was so convinced that verse 4 has no authenticity that he omitted it from his translation. Many commentators have thought that John believed this superstition to be fact, but I find nothing to confirm John's belief in it. Rather, John included the superstition in his report because it is at the heart of the lesson of this story.

---

3   Volume 36, George R. Beasley-Murray, Word Books, Inc., 1987, p. 70.
4   See also the discussion in Metzger, 209.

The Man

There was a "certain man" (v. 5) at the Pool of Bethesda who had believed this superstition for thirty-eight years. For thirty-eight years this particular man had believed the superstition—with no result! For this man the healing ritual of Bethesda had become a way of life. Everyday he went to Bethesda and waited for an angel to stir the waters, hoping or half-hoping to be able to be first in the pool and be healed. But he never made it in first.

One day "Jesus saw him lying there" (v. 6). The Greek word translated *saw* (*eido, εἴδω*) "often denote(s) spiritual perception."[5] Of all the people crowding into Bethesda to receive a healing, Jesus spiritually perceived this one particular man. Of all the people at Bethesda waiting to be healed by the miraculous water, Jesus healed *only* this one certain man. That in itself seems a bit odd. Why this particular guy? Why not anyone else?

Why would Jesus pick out one particular man rather than another? Perhaps Jesus spiritually saw (*eido*) the man's need or his readiness or something. Jesus, as omniscient God, looked into the heart of this one certain man and saw through him, saw into him. The Lord sees the heart (Jeremiah 20:12). What did He see?

We can determine to some degree what Jesus saw by the question He asked the man. J.C. Ryle says that "the English language here fails to give the full force of the Greek. Jesus asked 'Hast thou a will?'"[6] The *Authorized Version* translated it, "Wilt thou be made whole?" (v. 6). To understand Jesus' question we must go back to verse 5 and determine the man's ailment as best we can.

The man suffered from *astheneia* (ἀσθένεια), which is a Greek word that indicates a general weakness or sickness. The New Testament use of this word is holistic, pertaining to the whole person, body and spirit. It is sometimes used to describe the "weaker sex" (1 Peter 3:7), Paul's "unimpressive" appearance in 1 Corinthians 2:3, and the "weakness of the flesh" of Matthew 26:41. In Matthew 26 Jesus reprimanded the disciples for sleeping in the garden, "The spirit indeed is willing, but the flesh is weak" (*asthenes,* ἀσθενὲς).

---

5 *Theological Dictionary of the New Testament*, abridged by Geoffrey W. Bromiley, Eerdmans Publishing, Grand Rapids, Michigan, 1992.
6 *John*, Volume 1, R.C. Ryle, p. 274.

No doubt the man at the Bethesda pool lived the lifestyle of an invalid. For thirty-eight years he had chased a chance for miraculous healing at Bethesda. He was caught in the grip of a superstition that dominated his life, but produced no satisfying result. Surely some physical ailment had caused this man to seek healing many years ago, when he first started going to Bethesda. And during the ensuing decades he undoubtedly acquired additional ailments as a result of age and the adapted patterns of life that were undoubtedly part of that scene.

We all do this to one degree or another. We all become like the people we are with, whether we adapt to them or are simply attracted to people like ourselves. Birds of a feather do flock together. And this man had fellowshiped with the lame, with those who believed this superstition for thirty-eight years. If we know nothing else about the man, we can be pretty sure that he believed this superstition because he lived it for thirty-eight years.

Jesus saw in this man a common weakness that was in need of the strength and healing of the Holy Spirit. Jesus saw that this man's weakness (*astheneia*) could be strengthened by the Holy Spirit. Jesus may have chosen this particular man because he well-represented those who had been caught in this particular superstition. To heal this man in the way that Jesus healed him would show the others how they, too, could be healed.

The Miracle

Jesus asked him, "Wilt thou be made whole?" (*Authorized Version*). I hear indignation in Jesus' voice as He asked the question. *Do you even want to be healed?* The question accused the man of not really wanting health and wholeness. Healing would upset his adapted lifestyle. His life would change if he were healed, and change is often hard for people, and particularly hard for people who are stuck in a rut, captured by bad habits.

People often get stuck in the lifestyles of their sin and develop sin related diseases. Diseases are often fed by the lifestyles people live. And too often people live particular lifestyles hoping to reap some benefit from the ailment they claim. Like a person on welfare, a vicious cycle of behavioral justification can take over people's lives. Sometimes it is easier to be sick than to be healthy.

I imagine this man had made a life of begging and receiving charity, and to some extent was caught in such a vicious cycle. In fact, I think that this is the context of the miracle that provides the lesson it teaches. This guy had learned how to beg, and we can assume that after thirty-eight years he was able to make a living of it. It probably didn't provide much, but enough. Over time it became a reliable skill. He learned where to be, how to dress, what to say in order to evoke the guilt that would produce the alm. At some point, it probably became his only way to make a living. After thirty-eight years he believed he could do little else. So, he took charity because Temple goers practiced charity.

Jesus then came along and asked him if he *wanted* to be healed. Note that the man didn't answer the question that Jesus asked him. Rather, he responded with his belief that his problem was someone else's fault.

"It's not my problem," he said. "I have no one to help me."

But that was not an answer to the question that Jesus asked. Jesus inquired about him, about his own willingness to be healed, not about his friends. Jesus asked him if *he* was willing to be healed, and he answered that he had no friends to help him. He deflected Jesus' question about the state of his own heart, suggesting that his problem was that he had no friends.

The man was ill, weak, even sick after thirty-eight years of playing this game of "it's not my fault." Can you hear the righteous indignation in Jesus' voice? I can feel His frustration, not just with this particular man, but with the whole situation at Bethesda—the spider web of superstition that had been woven around this drainage pool, and its sanction by the Temple establishment.

Jesus saw the man in the crowd and pressed him, *Do you want to stay here all your life!?* The man didn't answer the question, but avoided the issue Jesus raised by blaming someone else for his situation.

"I have no one to help me," he replied.

The Command

"Rise," said Jesus (v. 8). And he did. The fact that he rose suggests that there had been nothing keeping him from rising before Jesus saw through him and commanded him to rise. Of course, there is a miracle involved in his rising. But it may not be that the medical condition of his legs miraculously changed. Rather, the spiritual condition of his heart may have miraculously changed. After all, Jesus wasn't aiming at his legs, He was aiming at his heart.

One of the definitions of *egeiro* (ἐγείρω, rise) is "to arouse from the sleep of death." It means to cause to wake up. *Rise and shine*, Jesus commanded the man. *Wake up and smell the coffee!*

Jesus added to this command, "take up your bed and walk." *Airo* (take up) means to remove. The sense of Jesus' command was: *Remove yourself! Get your things and get out of here!*

The final verb Jesus used, *peripateo* (περιπατέω), is a compound verb most often translated as *walk*, but also means *to be occupied*. To be occupied means to make one's way, to progress or to make due use of opportunities. Jesus commanded the man to get up, get out, and make something of himself, to occupy himself in some other way.

And that is exactly what the man did. He got up and left. Was he filled with warm and fuzzy feelings? Or did he leave because he had been caught cheating his own life.

The Lesson

What have I done to the miracle of Bethesda? Has the miracle simply been explained away with this interpretation? Not at all! The miracle was that the man obeyed the Lord's command. The real miracle was obedience to Christ and the healing that comes from simple obedience. The miracle was that the hard edge of God's truth kicked this particular man out of his habituated comfort zone. It was not a *warm, fuzzy, violin sawing on the heartstrings of sentimentality* kind of miracle. Rather, it was more of an *"Oh shit! I've been discovered. I'd better get outta' here"* kind of miracle. But it was a bona fide miracle nonetheless.

The miracle has not been destroyed at all. Rather, it has been made all the more real because it is no longer a silly superstition about being touched by Jesus' magic wand. The Jesus' magic wand interpretation confuses the superstition with the reality. It turns Jesus into the same kind of miracle worker that superstitions feed on. But Jesus was out to break the superstitions that had enslaved humanity, not to further them.

The miracle at Bethesda was the work of God's grace and the power of the Holy Spirit. The miracles of the gospel are always a matter of the grace of obedience, not the magic of superstition. Remember, not everyone at Bethesda was healed, just this one certain man. God chose to heal only him. And he was healed by God's grace through obedience to Christ, through faith. To be awakened to the truth, to believe the truth is what faith is all about.

The miracle of that healing, the miraculous healing of God's grace through obedience to Christ, is readily available to all of God's people. Of course, it doesn't always give you what you expect, or what you want. But it does serve God's purpose, and that is enough for God's people. What else could a Christian want than to be in service to God's purpose?

This understanding of the miracle at Bethesda is consistent with Jesus' teaching regarding miracles and the gospel He preached. It proclaims the truth to those who have lost the truth, and is the result of the miraculous work of the Holy Spirit by the grace of God. The miracle at Bethesda is a classic example of Jesus' teaching that the gospel is not a matter of superstitious magic, but of the grace of obedience to Christ.

In this light, the gospel shines clearly in the Bethesda story, though it runs counter to our expectations. Shouldn't we expect the miracles of Jesus to surprise us? Don't God's miracles overturn human expectations? Shouldn't Christianity put an end to superstition? The answer is yes, yes and yes! And the story of Bethesda is not yet over.

No More

"And at once the man was healed, and he took up his bed and walked. Now that day was the Sabbath. So the Jews said to the man who had been healed, 'It is the Sabbath, and it is not lawful for you to take up your bed.' But he answered them, 'The man who healed me, that man said to me, "Take up your bed, and walk."' They asked him, 'Who is the man who said to you, "Take up your bed and walk"?' Now the man who had been healed did not know who it was, for Jesus had withdrawn, as there was a crowd in the place. Afterward Jesus found him in the temple and said to him, 'See, you are well! Sin no more, that nothing worse may happen to you.' The man went away and told the Jews that it was Jesus who had healed him. And this was why the Jews were persecuting Jesus, because he was doing these things on the Sabbath. But Jesus answered them, 'My Father is working until now, and I am working.' This was why the Jews were seeking all the more to kill him, because not only was he breaking the Sabbath, but he was even calling God his own Father, making himself equal with God."—John 5:9-18

We have just witnessed the first three miracles in the gospel of John. With these miracles Jesus gave a particular teaching about the relationship between miracles and gospel. He said that the gospel was not dependent upon miracles, that receiving the gospel was not a matter of experiencing some kind of magic miracle. He didn't deny the reality of supernatural events, nor that He could cause them. But He made a point of telling us that the desire for miracles distracts people from the heart of the gospel.

At the wedding at Cana of Galilee Mary wanted Jesus to turn the water into wine because they had run dry. Jesus responded, "Woman, what does your concern have to do with Me?" (John 2:4). The miracle had nothing to do with Jesus' ministry. The story appears so that Jesus could teach that the gospel is not a matter of miracle working. And yet He worked the miracle.

When Jesus healed the nobleman's son (John 4:46-54) He rebuked him, lamenting, "Unless you people see signs and wonders, you will by no means believe." People clamored for signs and wonders, but Jesus wanted faith. And yet Jesus met the nobleman's desire for the healing of his son. But He was adamant that the miracle was given, not for the sake of the man's son, but for the nobleman's faith and for the faith of Jesus' followers, those who witnessed it, and those who would read about it, for you and me.

At Bethesda Jesus healed only this one certain man, again, not for his own sake, but for the watching world. By healing this one man Jesus broke the hold that a particular Temple superstition had upon the lame and infirm. The healing of this one certain man lanced the boil of superstition that trapped "a great multitude of sick people" (John 5:3).

There was much more at stake than one man's ability to walk. The stakes had been raised significantly when this one particular man began to walk (*peripateo*). This man began walking, not just by putting one foot in front of the other, but in the sense of "walking the walk and talking the talk." This man had seen the light. The Lord said "go," and he went.

When he got up and began walking the walk, the Bethesda miracle took on a different character. The healing of this one certain man bumped smack into the Jewish Temple establishment in a most powerful and unique way. The meaning of this parable took on a social dimension that it didn't have before the man began to walk in faith.

The Sabbath

Have you ever wondered why the Jews accused Jesus of Sabbath violation when He healed this man? Doesn't that seem like an odd accusation? What did the healing of this one certain man have to do with the Sabbath? The Jewish establishment's concern that this incident happened on the Sabbath is completely out of place unless we understand that the Temple authorities were out to get Jesus on any charge they could. Carrying a bedroll—a burden—was indeed a technical violation of the Pharisaic Sabbath. But if we understand burden to mean only a bedroll, it seems a very trivial violation. To not carry a burden on the Sabbath meant to not carry on worldly business or to engage in personal concerns. The reason that this healing rang the Sabbath bell lies in the nature of the man's illness, the method of his healing, and the implications for the Temple as the Bethesda pool was revealed to be what it actually was—a silly superstition that preyed upon the weak and infirm.

It is unlikely that the Jews thought that Jesus was going to put the medical industry out of business by healing all the sick people in Jerusalem. He had healed only this one certain man. He could have healed all the sick people at Bethesda, but He didn't. That fact alone suggests that Jesus' did not intend to eliminate sickness. The healing wasn't about ending sickness. It was about ending Temple superstitions. It wasn't about the man, it was about the Temple.

The purpose of this healing miracle had little to do with this particular man, although he benefited greatly from it. Rather, the purpose of this healing miracle was to break the bond of ignorance and superstition that bound people to a false understanding of God and reality. This miracle both exposed and revealed the real miraculous, supernatural working of God's grace through the simple obedience of faith.

Jesus wanted to demonstrate that miracles were the result of obedience to God—obedience alone to God alone through faith alone in Jesus alone based upon Scripture alone. Not that obedience produces miracles. Jesus is not into works-righteousness. But that grace produces obedience, which produces miracles. Grace is the horse that pulls the cart of obedience.

Real miracles were never like the magical, superstitious stories of an ignorant and spiritually blind people striving to be first in the pool. Superstitions like the story about Bethesda's healing water served only to keep people from the health and blessings that God intends them to have. Superstition binds people to a superstitious understanding of God that is not true. It blinds people to the grace of God.

In contrast, all of the miracles of Jesus sprang from the grace of faith, of trust, of obedience. Jesus' miracles opposed and corrected the many superstitions that had enslaved God's people. All of the miracles of Jesus turned people to faithfulness, to simple obedience to God.

The blind, lame, and withered people waiting for the stirring of the Bethesda waters had been caught in a cycle of weakness (*astheneia*) and poverty centered around this healing superstition, a false belief. The superstitious belief in the restorative powers of holy water kept people in weakness and poverty. It also served to support the power of the Temple and its corruption by catering to the ignorance of superstition and magic.

The superstitious belief that the waters of Bethesda could heal was related to the ritual of Temple sacrifice, the ritual that Christ had come to end. Although not a formal part of the Temple program, the pool at Bethesda fed the superstitious beliefs of Temple magic and thereby supported the political power of the priests. Such superstitious beliefs gave the Temple priests prestige and political power among the ignorant. Unfortunately the prevailing political system was a rotten mess of religious patronage.

The last command of Jesus to the man who had been healed was *walk (peripateo)*, which, as we know, can also be translated *be occupied*. Jesus commanded the man to find some other way to sustain himself. In other words—Jesus told him to get a life!

The man was healed immediately, and immediately rose, took up his bed and walked. He began immediately to do what Jesus commanded—*peripateo*. He got a life. He changed his occupation. But it was the Sabbath, and that was the rub.

The man immediately began walking in faith, networking for opportunities to escape his dependence upon charity. That was the activity that caught the notice of the Pharisees who had been watching Jesus. Like a small town Southern cop who has pulled over a speeder with a decidedly Northern accent, the Jews began to hassle the healed man with legal technicalities, especially when he turned up in the Temple.

The Problem

Looking toward charging Jesus with blasphemy, the Pharisees wanted to know the identity of the person who had healed the man. *Was He the Son of God?* they asked. They were well aware of the stories and rumors in circulation, and of the scope of the Messianic predictions. They hoped to gather some evidence to use against Jesus. But the poor man had been so overwhelmed by his healing and his new life that he honestly didn't know who had healed him. He only knew the result of his obedience, his new faith. He had a new life, and that was enough.

Meanwhile, Jesus had melted into the crowd at the feast. Later, Jesus and this man met again in the Temple. Jesus commented upon his healing. I see "you have been made well" (*hugies, ὑγιής*), He said (v. 14). *Hugies* means whole, well, or sound, and carries the sense of conformity to the truth. In essence Jesus said, *I see you have conformed your life to the truth.* Then Jesus said to the man, "sin no more" (v. 14).

Nowhere in this story has the word or idea of sin been employed. Up to this point the man's ailment had been described as illness, weakness—not sin. But here Jesus suggested that the man's problem all along had been sin, not illness.

The phrase, "sin no more" also occurs in John 8:11. Jesus used it there with the woman caught in adultery. The difference was that the woman was actually caught in sin. The woman's sin was obvious. She was plainly a sinner.

But why did Jesus say "sin no more" to the Bethesda man? Why did Jesus choose these words to say to a man who had been incapacitated for thirty-eight years, an invalid? The answer is obvious, but because it doesn't fit the usual explanation of this miracle, people don't see it.

The obvious truth is that Jesus did not think the man had been all that sick. Rather, Jesus understood him to be a sinner. He was not weak and withered from illness, but from sin, from falsehood, from living a lie. The man had lacked a proper connection with God and with God's truth. Whatever else was wrong with him, this was at its root. The problem was moral, not biological.

It is Jesus' observation of the man's sin that has given rise to my particular understanding of the Bethesda story. Jesus had spiritually seen (*eido*) at the outset that this certain man didn't have a problem with illness, but with sin. Jesus *saw* through him. He *saw* the lie this man was living.

The man's life had not been in conformity with the truth. He had been living a lie. After thirty-eight years it had become an unconscious lie. That is, the man had convinced himself that the lie he lived was true. He had been caught up in it for so long that he literally had no way out of it. He was stuck, and Jesus freed him. His lie had been like a crutch that kept the man from walking right, and Jesus kicked it out from under him. And the man got up and walked away from his sin.

The Larger Problem

The difficulty was that the man's new walk of faith bumped into the Sabbath practices dictated by the Pharisees. It revealed a larger lie at the heart of the Temple. Jesus didn't want to eliminate the Sabbath or the Sabbath proscriptions, only to free people from domination by legalistic Sabbath dictates that had come from self-righteous men, not God. Jesus wanted the real Sabbath observance to serve God. The Sabbath had been taken hostage by Jewish legalists. The Pharisees used the Sabbath to force adherence to a legalistic religious system in which they were the top benefactors.

The rub came because the freedom that Jesus gave to the man He healed threatened that system. It showed it to be false. The Jews believed that any attack upon or deviation from their Sabbath laws amounted to a personal attack upon them. And they "sought all the more to kill him" (v. 18).

Jesus had freed the Bethesda man and called him to get up, get out and sin no more. But as the man moved away from his sin and the religious system that kept him in it, he also moved away from the Sabbath as interpreted and dictated by the Pharisees. Jesus had made an example of this one particular man, and his example, his healing, his freedom in Christ, his freedom from superstition threatened the establishment of the Temple.

The healed man had captured the attention of the people and the people had captured the attention of the Pharisees. The Pharisees then found Jesus to be the source of the healing, the source of what they saw to be a problem.

Jesus' then turned His attention to the Pharisees who had been watching Him. Now that He had their attention, He had much to tell them.

Verily, Verily

"So Jesus said to them, 'Truly, truly, I say to you, the Son can do nothing of his own accord, but only what he sees the Father doing. For whatever the Father does, that the Son does likewise. For the Father loves the Son and shows him all that he himself is doing. And greater works than these will he show him, so that you may marvel. For as the Father raises the dead and gives them life, so also the Son gives life to whom he will. The Father judges no one, but has given all judgment to the Son, that all may honor the Son, just as they honor the Father. Whoever does not honor the Son does not honor the Father who sent him.'" —John 5:19-23

The point of Jesus' miracles was to get people's attention. Jesus has a message, and the purpose of His miracles is to draw attention to His message. So, once Jesus got the attention of the Pharisees, He began with a double *amen*.

The word *amen* is a most remarkable word. In the Bible it was transliterated directly from the Hebrew into the Greek of the New Testament, then into Latin and into English and many other languages, so that it is practically a universal word. It has been called the best known word in human speech.

The word is directly related—and almost identical—to the Hebrew word *amam*, which means *believe* or *faithful*. It has come to mean *sure* or *truly*. It is an expression of absolute trust, agreement and confidence. Jesus began with a double *amen* in order to call attention to the fact that what He said next could be absolutely trusted as the whole truth and nothing but the truth.

Sure enough, the rest of chapter five contains some of the deepest of Jesus' teaching. He spelled out as clearly as language allows, who He is, His relationship with God, and what He has come to do. In this explanation He began with the doctrine of the Trinity, fully given for all to behold. The good news is that Jesus has given a full-orbed explanation of the deep things of God. The bad news is the poverty of human language to convey it and of the human intellect to understand it.

Jesus stretched language and human understanding to new heights, plumbing the depths of God. The doctrine of the Trinity is unique to Christianity. It is what makes Christianity Christian. It is what differentiates Christianity from all other religions, and it is a non-negotiable doctrine. Anything less than or other than Trinitarian theology is simply not Christian theology. It is an extremely important, complex, and subtle doctrine, but one that is absolutely foundational. Thus Jesus began with a double *amen*.

The Trinity

The essence of the Trinity is that in and through Jesus, God acts on behalf of God the Father and by means of His Holy Spirit. The mystery of God and the power of the Holy Spirit come together in Jesus, the Son of God. Father, Son, and Holy Spirit act in harmony and unity, yet each is a distinct, separate Person. Christianity cannot be understood apart from the Trinity.

When Jesus said that "the Son can do nothing of Himself" (v. 19) He didn't mean that He was weak or impotent of Himself, only that all of His actions had the accompanying authority of God and the power of the Holy Spirit. His action was commensurate with God's action. The Son and the Father act in unison and in harmony.

The Pharisees correctly surmised that He intended to say that He was equal with God in power and authority. To the Jews, who were committed to the First Commandment, only two interpretations of Jesus' words were possible. Either Jesus was a madman, guilty of the highest blasphemy, or He was in fact the Son of God.

For the most part, the Jews did not expect the Messiah to be divine. Their monotheism does not allow such a thing. They expected a human savior or prophet to act in the political arena. Consequently, Jesus' claim of divine Sonship made Him greater than their expected Messiah. His claim went far beyond their highest expectation, and beyond what their monotheism could allow. The Jews can hardly be faulted for their initial doubt of such a claim.

The purpose of Trinitarian theology is to explain how Jesus can be the Son of God. In essence, Jesus told the Jews that if they wanted to argue with what He did or who He was, they would have to argue with God Himself because He—Jesus, the Son of God—was part and parcel of the universal Godhead. And that's a very large claim. It stands as a condemnation of every religion known to humanity, except Christianity. It stands as a clarification of the character of God Himself.

The application of this verse, this idea, is simple in conception and practice, but it terribly offends our worldly sensitivities. The application is that knowledge of God the Father is found in knowledge of the Son of God. We know that "knowledge (of God) is too wonderful for (us); it is high, (we) cannot attain unto it" (Psalms 139:6). Direct knowledge of God is beyond human reach. So, knowledge of God can only be found through knowledge of the Son. In other words, if you want to know about God, learn about His Son.

But the application extends even further. It goes on to say that we cannot know anything about God apart from knowledge of Jesus Christ. In fact, all knowledge of God that is not based upon Jesus Christ is ultimately false. The application is that if you want to know God, you must begin with Christ. There is no other way.

The First Commandment

Here Jesus addressed the First Commandment, "Thou shalt have no other gods before me" (Exodus 20:3). Jesus applied it to Himself, Thou shalt have no other gods before Him, meaning Jesus. When it sinks in that Jesus claims equality with God Almighty, we can begin to understand the difficulty the Jews had with Him. His exclusive claim is just as offensive today. Those schooled in multiculturalism and religious relativity today choke on Jesus' claims of divinity and of exclusivity.

The persistent application of this verse is that all religious understanding that does not issue from Jesus is false. All religions that do not correctly worship the Father, Son, and Holy Spirit through Jesus Christ are false religions. Misguided worship can easily violate the First Commandment. The application is that all who say, "Oh, I believe in God, but I don't need to worship Jesus Christ," are mistaken and self-deluded.

The application is that all who think that they can worship God just as well out in the woods, apart from the body of Christ (the church) are wrong, and their error may cost them eternal salvation. The application is that all who think that they know and respect Jesus, but who have no abiding relationship with Him, who do not honor their covenant with Him, are hell bound. The application of this verse is that

> "many will say to (Jesus) in that day, 'Lord! Lord! Did we not prophesy in Your name, and through Your name throw out demons, and through Your name do many wonderful works?' And then (Jesus) will say to them I never knew you! Depart from Me" (Matthew 7:22-23).

These are some of the implications of the doctrine of the Trinity, and they should help us to understand the consternation of the Jews.

Jesus went on to say in verse 20 that the works of God through the Son would be greater than any of God's works previously known, that the world would marvel at such future works, that Christianity would utterly change the world—and it has! Among the future works that He meant were those listed in the next verse: the raising of the dead, and the giving of life. Sure enough, Jesus' ministry went on to include the raising of the dead, and the giving of life.

For Christ, life itself emanates from the Father and people must maintain a proper relationship with the Father in order to live the life given by the Father. Stated negatively, people without a living relationship with God are dead—dead to God and dead to the things of God. In this regard, Jesus came to a dead world in order to resurrect it to life in God. People are dead without Christ! Only through Christ can people properly connect with God and receive the new life God has for them. There is no other way. If there is another way, Jesus is a terrible liar. But if He is correct, this is a very important teaching.

The New Life

The word translated *quickeneth* (v. 21, ζωοποιέω) in the *Authorized Version* literally means to make alive, as in giving birth. It is a very strong word in the sense that it is concrete and factual, and implies the power of making life of all kinds, both physical and spiritual.

To illustrate this point Jesus resurrected a few dead souls. But He did not resurrect all who were dead, nor did Jesus heal all those who were ill. He performed only a few such miracles to get our attention, and to teach us something terribly important. Through His miracles and the teaching that accompanied them, Scripture teaches that those who were not miraculously healed or resurrected can receive the same result through belief in and a personal relationship with Jesus Christ. They can be raised from living death and given new life through faith in Christ, through obedience to Christ.

Who can actually receive this life that Jesus gives? Who can be raised from the dead? Who can receive the benefits of resurrection and new life? Jesus said, "the Son gives life to whom He will" (v. 28). That means that the decision about who will be saved belongs to Jesus alone. Jesus will give life to whom He will because He alone is the judge of this world. The difference between heaven and hell is based upon the judgment of Christ. The decision is His.

Many people wonder why God doesn't just save everyone. After all, God claims to be loving. Will everyone ultimately be saved? Or only the elect? The question deserves a real answer, and requires a thorough reading of Scripture. Such a reading reveals that the major Scriptural issue is not why God doesn't save everyone, but why God chooses to save anyone.

Scripture says that "There is none righteous, no not one" (Romans 3:10). The real question isn't about universal salvation, but about salvation for any. Given the sinful condition of humanity, it is a wonder that anyone can be saved! The doctrine of grace isn't that God will save all, but that God will save any. By the grace of God some people are redeemed. To challenge this is to challenge the judgment of Jesus Christ.

Salvation is not for us to judge, but for Jesus. God "has committed all judgment to the Son" (v. 22). That means that your salvation is a personal matter between you and Jesus. Because salvation requires a personal relationship with Jesus, it is most appropriate that judgment belongs to Him. J.C. Ryle said,

> "There seems a fitness in this. He who was condemned by an unjust judgment, and died for sinners, is He whose office it will be to judge the world."[7]

Jesus went on to say that the honor of the Father requires the honor of the Son and visa versa. When Jesus said that "all should honor the Son just as they honor the Father" (v. 23) He drew an analogy to the Fifth Commandment, "Honor thy father and thy mother" (Exodus 20:12).

We teach our children that such honor is not merely thinking highly of mom and dad, but that such honor is primarily manifested through obedience. Just as mom and dad obey God, children should obey mom and dad. We honor our parents by obeying them. Of course, honor is more than obedience, but it begins with obedience and apart from obedience it doesn't begin at all.

Here again, as with Jesus' teaching regarding the miracles we have looked at so far, we find an emphasis upon obedience to God through Jesus Christ. The grace of God through Jesus Christ has not exempted anyone from perfect obedience to God's Law. Obedience is still necessary. But in the light of Christ, our imperfect obedience is made acceptable. The perfect obedience of Christ is applied to those in Christ whose obedience is imperfect—but only in Christ, only through Christ, only because of Christ.

In the Old Testament people had only one salvation method. They were to obey God's law. But they failed. The primary lesson of the Old Testament is the failure of the Jews to live in obedience to God's law.[8] With the advent of Christ and the New Testament, that salvation method has been perfected. Now, those in Christ have Christ's perfect obedience and the ultimate atonement for sin, paid for on the cross, applied to them. Because Christ has done what no human being can do, all people are free to live in obedience to Jesus Christ, trusting in the hope that God will bring to fruition what He

---

7 *John*, Volume 1, R.C. Ryle, Banner of Truth Trust, Carlisle, Pennsylvania, 1869, 1987p. 289.
8 *God's Great Plan For The World*, Phillip A. Ross, Pilgrim Platform, Marietta, Ohio, 2019.

began. To receive God's Son is to honor God. To obey God's Son is to obey God. But only in Christ and only because of Christ.

This is the truth that offended the Jews. But we shouldn't single out the Jews in this regard because it offends people of every religion and every time, and people of no religion. It offends human pride. Indeed, that is its purpose! It clears the deck of all religious contenders, save Christ alone.

Hear and Believe

"Truly, truly, I say to you, whoever hears my word and believes him who sent me has eternal life. He does not come into judgment, but has passed from death to life. Truly, truly, I say to you, an hour is coming, and is now here, when the dead will hear the voice of the Son of God, and those who hear will live."

—John 5:24-25

Jesus began this monologue in verse 19 with the words, *Amen, amen* (or *truly, truly*) in order to alert His hearers that what followed was absolutely true and could be trusted. In verse 24 he repeated those words, alerting the faithful with a second double *amen*. The first double *amen* called attention to the doctrine of the Trinity, teaching that God the Father acted in unison and harmony with Jesus Christ the Son, through the power of the Holy Spirit. The first double *amen* established the authority, source, and power of Jesus.

This second double *amen* now alerts us to the nature of the action begun in Jesus Christ. We learned in verse 21 that "the Son gives life to whom He will" because "the Father ... has committed all judgment to the Son." In other words, Jesus alone determines who receives new life and salvation—and who receives damnation. Again, your salvation is a personal matter between you and Jesus.

But lest we should think that salvation is bestowed arbitrarily, we now learn that Jesus has established a partner in judgment. Judgment, which results in either salvation or damnation, is not simply dependent upon the whims of Jesus (as if Jesus had whims, which He doesn't). Rather, Jesus has decreed that

> "he who hears (His) word and believes in (God) who sent (Him) has everlasting life" (v. 24).

It is Jesus who determines who is saved, and now we see that Jesus has determined that those who hear His word and believe in the Triune God are those to be saved (Romans 10:14).

The Hearing

When Jesus said that salvation belongs to those who hear, he meant more than those who simply listen. The Greek word for *hear*, *akouo*, also means *attend*, *understand*, and *learn*. The kind of hearing that Jesus meant requires a particular response. It is possible to hear something and misunderstand, reject, or ignore it. But that's not what Jesus had in mind. J.C. Ryle said,

> "It means hearing with the heart, hearing with faith, hearing accompanied by obedient discipleship."[9]

The response that Jesus requires is obedience. To hear His word is to obey it, to make it central in your life. Anything less than obedience indicates the failure to actually hear Him. Jesus doesn't force anyone to obey. All obedience to Christ must be voluntary. It must proceed from the heart and will of the believer, or not at all. Christians must *want* to obey Christ.

Jesus wasn't satisfied with mere hearing. He added the requirement to believe, "he who hears My word *and believes*" (v. 24—emphasis added). Had He instructed the faithful to hear or obey alone, people might think that salvation is a matter of mere obedience, of performance. That would make salvation a matter of human action, and people might think that heaven could be had by the power of human will alone. Were salvation only a matter of obedience, people could obey themselves into heaven. But the Jews of the Old Testament proved the folly of that approach. They had God's Word (the Ten Commandments), but could not obey (or hear) God's Word. God's law alone is insufficient.

---

9 Ryle, p. 295.

Jesus added belief—*pisteuo*. People can obey by an act of their own will. People can choose to obey. But belief is another matter altogether. One cannot simply choose to believe something. And if they could, that's not the kind of belief Jesus has in mind. Rather, belief issues from discernment, understanding, and life experience. Belief is not a function of the will, will is a function of belief. In the case before us belief requires the presence of the Holy Spirit because people cannot simply decide to understand the gospel. The gospel is repugnant to humanity because it shows us that what we consider to be our most unique and important attributes as human beings is repugnant to God. We pride ourselves on what offends God—self reliance.

People either understand the gospel or they don't. People have either experienced the Holy Spirit or they haven't. People have either been convicted by God's truth or they haven't. We can choose to be open to God before the truth of the gospel has been revealed to us, but once it has been revealed we either get it or we don't. This does not mean that we understand it completely, comprehensively, or immediately. Rather, it means that the seed of faith has been received. We can be open to a change of heart, but we cannot make God act. We cannot change our own hearts any more than we can love what we hate, or hate what we love by the mere strength of our own will.

Belief in Jesus issues from the presence of the Holy Spirit in the lives of believers. Belief comes by the grace of God. It is not something that people can work up on their own. In this regard, belief in God is the result of the presence and power of the Holy Spirit.

Jesus didn't call for a vague or undetermined faith, as if any sort of faith would do. People sometimes talk as if the gospel means to have faith in faith (or faith in the power of belief itself), as if the act of believing in something—anything!—constitutes Christian faithfulness. Jesus requires not mere faith, but faith in God. In particular, faith in the Triune God that He had just described. It is not unfocused faith that saves, but faith in God as Father, Son, and Holy Spirit. Human faith (believing) doesn't do the saving. God does the saving. The correct object of faith is critical because it is God, the object of our faith, who does the saving.

The Response

By requiring that people "believe in (God) who sent Him" (v. 24), Jesus also tells us that He is on a mission. In this phrase the authority of the gospel is confirmed. The gospel came from God and was not invented by men. He reiterated in John 7:16 and again in John 14:10 that the gospel is not His, but God's. Jesus, as the Son of Man, was a man under authority.

> "'He who hears My word,' He said, 'and believes *in Him who sent Me* has everlasting life" (v. 24—emphasis added).

Every word of the Lord is filled with meaning and truth. By using the present tense of *has* (*echo*) Jesus taught that the eternal life that is bestowed upon those who hear begins the moment they believe. Eternal life is not just some future state in the life hereafter—although it is that, too! Eternal life begins here on earth. It begins with belief. The Kingdom of God "operates in reality and power among men in this present age."[10] The everlasting life that comes with belief is the leading edge of the Kingdom of God.

> "Thy kingdom come, thy will be done, on earth as it is in heaven" (Matthew 6:10).

The Application

What is the application of this? Those who hear and believe will not come into Judgment (*krisis*). *Krisis* is most often translated as *judgment*, and we usually understand it as the negative aspects of judgment. We will all come before Christ in judgment. However, some will receive mercy and some damnation. It is the damnation side of judgment that is normally indicated by *krisis*. The *Authorized Version* translates the word as *condemnation*.

Romans 14:10 tells us that "all shall stand before the judgment seat of Christ." None will escape judgment, but some will escape condemnation. How? Some will receive mercy and salvation. That should provide ample incentive for making every effort to hear Jesus. This is the key to heaven itself. Hearing opens a person to the possibility of belief. Without hearing there can be no belief, but at the

---

10 *Articles of Affirmation and Denial on the Kingdom of God*, Dr. Jay Grimstead, editor, Coalition on Revival, P.O. Box A, Sunnyvale, CA, 94087, 1989, article 4.

same time without belief there can be no hearing. Which comes first hearing or belief? The answer is that the Holy Spirit comes first because it is the Holy Spirit who both brings the Word to be heard, and who changes the heart, which allows the hearing to happen.

Finally, verse 24 tells us that those who hear Jesus and believe in the Triune God who sent Him pass from death into life. Most commentators agree that Jesus is talking about spiritual death and spiritual life here. It was not that Jesus cannot raise people from physical death, He can. And has! But Jesus did not come to short circuit the lawfulness of God's world by miraculous intervention. He came to fulfill and complete God's world by bringing the gospel of salvation, and to establish the authority of God's Kingdom on earth.

The establishment of the Kingdom on earth requires men and women to be alive to the Spirit in Christ. But because people were not alive to the Spirit, it would also require the resurrection of many spiritually dead people. Without Christ people are dead. Like condemned criminals waiting execution, those without Christ are simply waiting for the ax to fall. The execution order has been given, and they are simply waiting on death row. Such are the living dead without Christ. But when Christ speaks and they hear—and believe, the execution order is canceled. Life is given to them once again. The captives are released!

However, this new life in Christ is not merely a legal matter of one's position before Christ the Judge. There are legalities and legal ramifications, of course. But the miracle is the accompanying change in the person's character upon hearing the pardon. Like the prodigal son, who "was dead and is alive" (Luke 15:24), the forgiven receive a new lease on life. The believer is different than s/he was without the forgiveness of Christ. And the proof of the reality of the belief is the fruit that it produces in the life of the believer.

The Dead Will Hear

Verse 25 begins with yet another double *amen*, confirming again that we are in the midst of some very important material. Jesus has described who will be saved (those who hear and believe), and how they will be resurrected (by not coming into condemnation, but passing from death into life). Verse 25 then assures the faithful that

God's Kingdom has indeed come already ("and now is"), and will continue into the future ("the hour is coming").

How will the dead hear? Making the dead hear is both the purpose of all miracles, and is the only miracle that makes any difference. People hear God's Word by the presence and power of the Holy Spirit, and the fruit of that hearing is obedience to the Word of God. This prediction was fulfilled with the conversion of many souls during Jesus' ministry, and fulfilled again at Pentecost when Jesus was preached to the Gentiles by His apostles.

> "And that day about three thousand souls were added to them" (Acts 2:41).

The dead (*nekros*), those destitute of vitality and power, will hear (*akouo*) the gospel by the miraculous grace of God. Understanding comes through obedience. From obedience then comes greater belief (*pisteuo*). We can also say that the dead come to life by the power and presence of the Holy Spirit, who gives them ears to hear. And when they hear the Word of God they believe, and out of that belief comes obedience. It seems to work both ways.

The difficulty with regard to the application of this verse is that people don't know that they are dead until they receive new life in Christ. It is by comparison that their new condition in Christ reveals their former condition without Christ. Apart from new life in Christ, the old life without Christ seems to be adequate. Apart from new life in Christ people are completely unaware of their own moral decay and spiritual poverty.

Apart from the reality of Christ, the effort of faithfulness is futile. Generic faith is futile. The self-effort to prop up generic Christless faith relentlessly fails to produce life. Enthusiasm evaporates, leaving a dry, crusty residue. People hide behind memories warped by time and false hopes. People hide behind the rationalization that they have matured beyond the need for spiritual discipline, like the five-year-old who speaks of the time when he was a little boy.

The sure evidence of such spiritual death is the lack of interest in Bible study and prayer, and in fellowship with the faithful. Spiritual death masquerades as innate human goodness. When I believe that I am basically a good person, and that God cannot reject me because of my goodness or my church attendance or my generosity or my character, I have reached the pinnacle of spiritual death. It is a natural process and everyone apart from Christ is caught up in it.

But a day is coming, an hour is coming when the living dead will hear the voice of God in Christ. Indeed, that day began with the advent of Christ. Christ has come, and that day is upon us. Let us work and pray for Christ's voice to be heard clearly, that many will hear and live.

Come Forth

"For as the Father has life in himself, so he has granted the Son also to have life in himself. And he has given him authority to execute judgment, because he is the Son of Man. Do not marvel at this, for an hour is coming when all who are in the tombs will hear his voice and come out, those who have done good to the resurrection of life, and those who have done evil to the resurrection of judgment. I can do nothing on my own. As I hear, I judge, and my judgment is just, because I seek not my own will but the will of him who sent me." —John 5:26-30

What makes it so difficult to give our brokenness to God is that so many people think that God has caused their brokenness, or that God aggravates it. But I assure you that God has not caused human brokenness (or sin). This mistaken belief occurs because God's Word points out human sin and brokenness. God wants people to draw near for healing, but in drawing near the brightness of God's light shines in the sin-darkened corners of the human spirit and reveals the sin and brokenness that is already there.

As God's light reveals human sin, many people find that the light aggravates it. Sure, seeing our sin is painful. Getting caught in our own lies is embarrassing. The natural consequence of exposure to the light of Christ is to pull away from what seems to cause the pain and discomfort. However, the light is not the cause, but the first step of healing. Revealing the existence of a thing is not the same as causing it.

The withdrawal from God really only serves Satan, who is the real cause of sin. Because the light of Christ provides healing, withdrawal from that light is a movement back toward sin. The natural reaction to the light of Christ sends people into a vicious cycle of sin and withdrawal from God because of their fear to receive God's healing. People naturally fear change, and real change is the most scary. Apart from God's supernatural intervention—miracles, we are stuck with our natural reaction.

God has given His Holy Spirit to serve as a supernatural defense against withdrawal from the brightness of God's light. The light that reveals human sin also heals it. To bear the intensity of the light we must receive the counterbalancing comfort and edification of the Holy Spirit. In doing so we will discover that prolonged exposure to God's light has a healing effect upon body and soul.

Verse 26 tells us that God has life in Himself. God is different than human beings in this regard. People do not have life in themselves. People are not self-sufficient, but are dependent upon many things—air, water, food, weather, one another, etc. But the most important of the human dependencies is the dependency upon God. The First Commandment requires our primary dependence upon God. To depend upon any other thing first and foremost is idolatry. People do not have life in themselves, but only in God is there real life, fullness of life.

God alone is self-sufficient, and because of the character of the Trinity, so is Jesus. God has given Jesus the same self-sufficiency as He has, because Jesus is His son. Therefore, just as people only have fullness of life in God, they also have fullness of life only in Christ. We can say both *only in God* and *only in Christ* because of the reality of the Trinity. We can also say *only by the power and presence of the Holy Spirit*, as well.

THE SON

The fact that all judgment has been given to the Son (v. 22) is repeated in verse 27. Its repetition is a sign that Jesus wanted to make sure that we heard it. God "has given (Jesus) authority to execute judgment" (v. 22). Why? Because He is the Son of Man. He knows us because He is a human being, and He knows God because He is a member of the Trinity.

The reference to the *Son of Man* here rather than to the *Son of God* is significant. There is much oscillation between referring to Jesus as the Son of Man and the Son of God. But here we see that judgment has been given to the Son of Man precisely because the Son of God humbled Himself to become a man, to put on flesh and experience what men experience, to know what we know and as we know. Jesus has been given the responsibility of judgment because He has become one of us. He knows human weakness and human strength. Therefore, He is in a position to judge rightly.

"Do not marvel at this," Jesus said in verse 28. Marvel at what? It is an important question because in verse 20 Jesus said that He would perform godly works greater than the miracles He had thus far performed "that (we) may marvel." He will perform works for us to marvel at (v. 20), but now cautions His hearers *not* to marvel at *this* (v. 28). So, what is *this* that we are not to marvel at, compared to the greater works at which we are to marvel?

The general subject Jesus addresses here is resurrection. He is discussing resurrection in the context of miracles because resurrection is miraculous. This teaching is given largely in response to all the people that Jesus had thus far encountered in His ministry who clamored for miracles. We are looking at Jesus' response to this desire for miracles.

The Soul

Thus far the people Jesus encountered have been overly concerned with petty miracles that effect mere maladies of the body. At Cana Jesus' mother thought it appropriate to make miraculous wine to quench the thirst of some friends at a wedding party. Later a nobleman was concerned about the bodily affliction of his son, who admittedly was "at the point of death" (John 4:47), but not dead. Nowhere do we find that the nobleman was concerned for the soul of his son, only his body. Jesus then healed the ailing boy and resurrected the dead soul of the nobleman.

Thus far people had not been concerned about the healing of the soul or the reality of eternal life. They simply wanted little body fixes to make them feel better. But Jesus had come not to fix the aches and pains of life, but to resurrect dead souls to eternal life. Of this verse Calvin writes,

> "Hence it arises that they pass by the resurrection of the soul with little concern, while the resurrection of the body excites in them greater admiration."[11]

Jesus was trying to move people from their self-concern to the greater concern about the salvation of humanity itself. Do not be concerned with these little body fixes that contribute nothing to the salvation of souls. He will extend this train of thought even to the raising of Lazarus. He will say, *do not marvel even at the resurrection of bodies*. Bodies in this world are healed and resurrected only to succumb once again to age and illness and death. Rather, marvel at the resurrection of dead souls to eternal life. But that is a story yet to come. Which is more difficult, to resurrect a body, or to resurrect a dead soul? Which is the better fix?

Jesus said, don't marvel at mere body centered miracles, for the time is coming for a greater miracle, when those in the graves—yes, the faithful who have died already, but also those who are walking memorials to their own dead souls—will hear His voice. Because the Kingdom of God is both a present and future reality in Christ, the resurrection of the dead is also both a present and future reality. Jesus has come to resurrect the walking dead.

This whole concept of the resurrection of the dead is a curious thing. First of all, resurrection is a miracle. Yet, people are overwhelmingly carnal and worldly. Consequently, what people perceive to be important are carnal and worldly things. People want their bodies fixed more than they want them resurrected.

One result of this fact is that the miracles we can see (body miracles) are easier to believe than the miracles we can't see (soul miracles, heart miracles). Perhaps this accounts for the believability of body miracles, such as healings and the bodily resurrection of the dead—as with Lazarus. People trust what they can see and distrust what they can't see. And yet,

> "faith is the assurance of things hoped for, the conviction of things not seen" (Hebrews 11:1).

---

11 *Calvin's Commentaries*, Volume XVII, Commentary on the Gospel of John, William Pringle, Translator, Baker Book House, Grand Rapids, MI, reprint 1993, p. 208.

We can see that a body that has been healed or resurrected, and so we believe more readily. But the resurrection of the soul, being beyond this life and beyond bodily perception, can't be seen—not here, not now. It is therefore more difficult to believe. Or is it?

As a matter of fact no one alive has ever seen a bodily resurrection. We can discount the rash of so-called beyond death experiences that populate contemporary media and bookstores. They are mere sensationalism and a sign of the spiritual confusion of our times. They may be more accurately described, as they are in the medical community, as near death experiences. But whatever you call them they are not resurrections. Jesus said,

> "If they do not hear Moses and the Prophets, they will not be persuaded, even though one rose from the dead" (Luke 16:31).

Even in the Bible there are very few actual bodily resurrections, that of Jesus being the most prominent and the most important. And lots of people saw the resurrected Christ, Paul being the last to see Him. But we need to understand that bodily resurrection is not biblically normative, not at the present time. It is not the norm for anyone or any group of people in the Bible. It is a future promise, not a present reality. Instances of actual resurrection are rare. They serve as teaching examples to point to a future hope and a spiritual reality. The future hope of bodily resurrection is the hope of eternal life in heaven and on earth as it is in heaven. In contrast, the spiritual reality this side of heaven is personal regeneration, or being born again (John 3:3). Regeneration is normative for Christians.

Jesus' teaching contradicts those who think that this world and the bodies that live in it are the all in all, that there is nothing beyond this life. Jesus' teaching contradicts those who think that there is no future and eternal heaven and hell. But Jesus also contradicts those who think that there is no present, bodily manifestation of resurrection. Jesus teaches that the present, bodily reality of resurrection is regeneration, being born again in Christ. The faithful are invited—commanded actually—to "come forth," to be born again. Those who hear, those who have ears to hear the command, do so.

The root produces the fruit. Here Jesus commands those who hear Him to produce the godly fruit of a godly root, just as those who fail to hear Him produce the godless fruit of a godless root. The godly root produces "resurrection of life," as the godless root produces "resurrection of condemnation" (v. 29). The Word of God unites God's people in the resurrection of life, but it also separates the godly from the godless in the resurrection of condemnation. God's Word both unites and divides.

Verse 30 refutes those who thought that Jesus was living and speaking in the flesh, as the Son of Man, as a mere mortal. Jesus assured His listeners that He is not governed by the flesh, that He does "not seek (His) own will but the will of the Father who sent (Him)." Even though God had relinquished all judgment to Jesus, Jesus did not judge of Himself, but submitted Himself to the judgment of God (through God's Word).

Here we see the Trinity in action. God gave all authority to Jesus, and Jesus submitted Himself to God's authority. Jesus the man and God the Spirit work in unison through the power of the Holy Spirit.

The principle here is the unity of God and Christ through the power of the Holy Spirit. The application of this principle comes through the Holy Spirit to bring regeneration to God's people so that they may also be in unity with God and with Christ in the Holy Spirit. The application is that there is no salvation apart from spiritual regeneration. Christian faith leads to rebirth. Those who are born again are then united in Christ, and divided or separated from the ungodly, from those who are not in Christ. Those born again in Christ are brought into unity with Christ through spiritual rebirth.

And herein lies Christian unity, the miraculous unity of the twice born. Praise be to God!

Testified Of Christ

"If I alone bear witness about myself, my testimony is not deemed true. There is another who bears witness about me, and I know that the testimony that he bears about me is true. You sent to John, and he has borne witness to the truth. Not that the testimony that I receive is from man, but I say these things so that you may be saved. He was a burning and shining lamp, and you were willing to rejoice for a while in his light. But the testimony that I have is greater than that of John. For the works that the Father has given me to accomplish, the very works that I am doing, bear witness about me that the Father has sent me. And the Father who sent me has himself borne witness about me. His voice you have never heard, his form you have never seen, and you do not have his word abiding in you, for you do not believe the one whom he has sent. You search the Scriptures because you think that in them you have eternal life; and it is they that bear witness about me, yet you refuse to come to me that you may have life. —John 5:31-40

Jesus had some powerful things to say, and in support of his right to say them He calls upon four witnesses. Only two witnesses were required by Jewish law. He brought to witness 1) His Father in heaven, 2) John the Baptist, 3) the miracles He had worked, and 4) the Scriptures. Each of these witnesses testified that He was the Christ, the promised Messiah of the Old Testament, the Son of God. There is plenty of evidence to convince the unbeliever of the truth of

Christ. But evidence has rarely made any difference to unbelievers. Unbelievers that care at all for genuine, objective evidence soon become converts.

> "Unbelief does not arise so much from want of evidence, as from want of will to believe."[12]

When Jesus declined to bear witness to Himself, He didn't mean to say that His witness was worthless, only that the self-witness of any man is biased. By definition a witness should be someone who stands apart from the event witnessed. No man is a reliable witness to his own testimony. Jesus simply acknowledged this reality.

Verse 32 calls attention to "another who bears witness of (Him)." Because the word *bears* occurs in the present tense we can surmise that Jesus means God the Father here, rather than John the Baptist. At this point, John would have been either in prison or dead. He was certainly dead when John wrote this. In either case, he would have *bore* witness (past tense), where God continues to *bear* witness.

In this same verse Jesus said, "and I know that the witness which He witnesses of Me is true." His use of the phrase *I know* must surely indicate that we can trust Jesus in this because He knows the Father intimately and personally. *Trust me,* Jesus said, *I know about this.* Jesus, unable to witness to His own veracity, witnesses to the truthfulness and trustworthiness of God.

It must be remembered here that Jesus was speaking to the Jews who had opposed and persecuted Him. In this context, He called John the Baptist to the witness stand. Earlier "The Jews sent priests and Levites from Jerusalem" (John 1:19) to question John when John had first appeared as a voice crying in the wilderness, "Prepare the way of the Lord" (Matthew 3:3). They went to John and inquired whether he was the Christ. No, he was not, he said. Was he Elijah? No. The Prophet? That is, did he consider himself to be the God-sent prophet for the times? No again. Well, "Who are you, that we may give an answer to those who sent us?" (John 3:22) they asked. John then testified to Jesus Christ, who would come after him, and whom they did not yet know.

---

12 Ryle, p. 302.

The point of all this is that Jesus reminded the Jews that they had believed John when he had said these things. And most assuredly the people had believed him. Because they believed John then, Jesus called him again to the witness stand. John bore witness to Jesus. They may have doubted God the Father because they did not know Him. But how could they doubt John, a flesh and blood real person whom they knew?

But the Lord God is not dependent upon the testimony of a mere man, and Jesus reminded them of this in verse 34. His Messianic claim did not depend upon John or upon any other man. Jesus simply reminded them of John's witness—not so much to prove His case but to open the way of salvation to them. Jesus' intention was to save those who hounded Him. Salvation builds upon belief. And if their belief could be strengthened by John's testimony, it would be all the better. But again, not for Jesus. He didn't need to prove anything. He simply wanted them to believe and be saved.

The Work

Jesus went on to testify to John as a great prophet, a "burning and shining lamp" (v. 35). Even the Jews had rejoiced in John's light —his preaching and ministry. They could not deny that John had an effective ministry, that he preached God's truth. Even if they didn't like John, they couldn't deny him because he was so beloved by the people. At the least they had to give public honor to John.

But you can take John or leave him, Jesus said, because I have "a greater witness than John's" (v. 35). His greater witness was the work which the Father had given Him, that in which He labored. Here Jesus points to His employment record with the Father. We often think of this in terms of His miracles, and they were certainly part of the work that Jesus accomplished. They should not be underestimated because the traditional, biblical understanding was that God worked miracles as a witness to His prophets. Four times in John's gospel Jesus appealed to His miracles to witness to Him, John 3:2, 5:35, 10:25 and 15:24.

The Old Testament is replete with miracles done to prove the veracity of God's prophets. The miracles of Jesus are undisputed, even by the Jews. They witnessed many miracles themselves and could not deny them. It is much easier for us in our day to deny them because we live so far away from them. But they were right there.

> "Unless the Jews could explain them away, they were bound, as honest and reasonable men, to believe our Lord's Divine mission."[13]

But the enemies of Christ could not discount His miracles. They could not explain them away, and neither can we. So they attributed them to Satan (see Matthew 12:26-28). They accused Jesus of being possessed by Satan, and of working miracles by the power of Satan. Jesus, of course, demolished this argument by showing them that Satan would not and could not cast himself out. To do so would put Satan at cross purposes with himself. It was not Satan who freed the demon possessed. It was God.

The Miracles

There are at least five things to note about the witness of Jesus miracles. 1) There were a lot of them. They weren't fluke occurrences, but were repeated at Jesus' will.

2) They were not minor, but great miracles. It's true that the nature of their greatness was not rightly understood. Most people thought the petty miracles to be great and completely missed the greater miracles within the lesser miracles. People thought that bodily healings were greater than the resurrection of the soul and regeneration in this life. The greatest of Jesus' miracles always had eternal ramifications. Those were the great miracles that testified to His divinity as the Son of God.

3) Jesus' miracles were public. He didn't hide them, but performed them in the open where all could see.

4) Jesus' miracles were works of love and mercy. They evidenced His compassion—genuine compassion, not the social niceties of making people feel better. Jesus' miracles were always beneficial to all, to the person healed and to those who witnessed them—even to those of us who read about them! They bring people to faith. They were never mere exhibitions of power. They were purposeful.

5) They appealed to the senses as well as the soul. There were always aspects of His miracles that were visible, touchable, visceral. Even though Jesus knew that the bodily aspects of miracles were less

---

13 Ryle, p. 310.

important than their effect upon the soul, He also knew that people were more inclined to enter into faith if they fixed on something sensible. People would come to appreciate the deeper aspects of His miracles as they grew in faith. But Jesus didn't hesitate to provide what people needed to come to faith. His miracles were not wrongly instituted, though Jesus was eager for people to grow beyond their childish attachments.

Finally, Jesus called God the Father to testify on His behalf. The Father's testimony has been an ongoing Scriptural and historical testimony. God would testify in the future, in the writing of the New Testament and in the lives of His people yet to come. But God had also testified in the past, through history and in the pages of the Old Testament.

The Jews

In spite of all of this, Jesus lamented, the Jews would not be able to receive the testimony of the Father because they were devoid of the presence of the Holy Spirit. This is both a statement of fact, and an indictment of their Spiritual poverty. They could not "hear" the testimony of the Father because they did not know Him. They had no personal relationship with God. The Holy Spirit did not inhabit or lead them. Consequently, they were without the help they needed to see the truth. Those without the presence of the Holy Spirit today are in the same situation.

This important theme is repeated throughout Scripture. John himself said in John 3:18,

> "He who believes in Him is not condemned; but he who does not believe is condemned already, because he has not believed in the name of the only-begotten Son of God."

John will also say later in 8:47,

> "He who is of God hears God's words; therefore you do not hear, because you are not of God."

James also said it in 1:21,

> "Therefore lay aside all filthiness and overflow of wickedness, and receive with meekness the implanted word, which is able to save your souls."

It is God's Word through the power of the Holy Spirit resident in the hearts and minds of God's people that facilitates the hearing of God which saves. Without Christ and the Triune Godhead—Father, Son, and Holy Spirit—manifest in God's Word, salvation would be impossible.

Jesus did not simply refer to all Jews in this indictment. Many Jews had come to faith. His disciples were mostly Jews. Rather, this indictment was made against those hardhearted and faithless people who deny the power of the Holy Spirit, who don't believe. Not just the Jews, but all who cannot hear the gospel in the plain words of Christ, all who fail to understand, who stand not under the grace of God in Christ, but under condemnation. There is no salvation apart from hearing the gospel. And there is no hearing of the gospel apart from personal regeneration.

Belief

Belief is not something that simply occupies your mind, like learning that George Washington was President and believing that he helped the country. While there are gospel facts to believe, belief itself is a matter of the soul. It requires repentance, justification, and regeneration. People must turn from their old ways, and receive the grace of God in Christ, and be born again by the power of the Holy Spirit. And I don't mean the charismania of being slain in the Spirit, or jumping up and down for joy, weeping, speaking in unknown languages, laughing yourselves silly, or barking like dogs.[14]

Spiritual birth is much more simple than all that. It requires no outward manifestation other than the confession of Christ and the fruit of a changed life. Period. Jesus brought a simple faith for a simple people. You don't need to be a rocket scientist to be a Christian. You don't need anything but faith alone in Christ alone through Scripture alone.

Belief is not a function of personal experience, though it produces personal experience. Paul said,

> "faith is the substance of things hoped for, the evidence of things not seen" (Hebrews 11:1).

---

14 https://wiki2.org/en/Toronto_Blessing

Things *not* seen, *not* experienced. Faith does not come by human power, not by having a religious experience. Responding to an altar call will not make you a Christian. Rather, faith comes through the work of God upon the hearts of His people. Certainly there are experiences of faith, but the experience does not come first. Faith comes first.

Jesus did not indite only those who don't worship in the fellowship of His Church, nor only those who fail to read their Bibles. He was talking to the *Jews*, to Pharisees, Sadducees, and Scribes—people who knew the Old Testament, people who read their Bibles. Jesus' indictment rests upon those inside the church as well as those outside. Many regular church goers (and church leaders as well) will fail the heavenly entrance exam—not because they don't know the right answers, but because they don't know Christ (Matthew 7:21-23).

When Jesus commanded His listeners to "search the Scriptures" in verse 39 He was talking about the Old Testament. But this admonition applies equally today to the whole of the Bible. Verse 39 carries two interpretations. First, Jesus admonished them for reading Scripture without the awareness of the Messiah that pervades the entire Old Testament. They read their Bibles, but failed to see Jesus in their reading. They mistakenly thought that eternal life was to be found in the doctrines of the Bible. Second, Jesus commanded them to search the Scriptures in order to find the witness that testified to Him.

Study

Notice that He didn't say *read* the Scriptures. He said *search*, pour over them thoroughly and diligently. Don't merely read them. Don't think you know them already. Study them. Here is where most modern people are as guilty as the ancient Jews. People hardly ever actually study their Bibles. There is very little real Bible study today. For the most part people think that the Bible is like a ticket to heaven, that all you have to do is to have one. People are content to listen to a Bible teacher talk, at church or on a monitor. People think that listening to someone else constitutes study.

The people in Jesus' day spent a lot of time listening to the Pharisees comment upon and interpret the Bible. But listening to others is not study. Even in school, if all you do is listen, you won't do well.

You have to crack the books yourself. And as far as that goes, reading books about Bible study is no better than listening to a lecture or watching a Bible teacher on TV. The content is the same. You consume warmed up leftovers from another person's study. In order to study the Bible, you must read and meditate upon it *yourself*. Don't take somebody else's word for what it says. You figure out what it says for yourself.

That doesn't mean that reading or listening to Bible teachers is bad. It's not. To think that you have to begin from scratch is just as much an error as believing that everything you read or hear about the Bible from others is true. Most people go from one extreme to the other, from not reading the Bible at all, to believing every new wind of doctrine that blows their way. Both are serious mistakes. The goal of Bible study is for *you* to understand God's Word for yourself—not *by* yourself, but *for* yourself. Each Christian must come to a personal understanding of Scripture, through a personal relationship with Christ.

But so many don't. So many people are comfortable with a spot for the family Bible on the fireplace. So many are happy just to come to church and to hear a word of encouragement and leave it at that. They don't want their lives disturbed by the truth, and they don't want to have to think about it because if that's all God means to them, they know that their future prospects are dim. They don't want to face *that* reality. They are happy with a Jesus who loves them just the way they are. They don't want to hear about the Lord who calls all people everywhere to repent, to change their ways, to conform to the image of Christ, to stop doing what makes them happy and start doing what makes God happy.

Eternal life is not found in the pages of the Bible (John 5:39). It's not found apart from the Bible, but neither is it *in* the Bible. Eternal life is found only in Christ Jesus, and Jesus is revealed in the Bible. To have the Bible without Christ is to be hopelessly lost. Just as to have Christ without the Bible is to have a Jesus of your own making.

Jesus put His finger on the heart of the problem in verse 40,

> "you are not willing to come to Me that you may have life."

It is not God's unwillingness to save everyone that is the truth of the gospel. The doctrine of election is not a matter of God's unwillingness. It is a matter of the stubborn unwillingness of sinners to admit the truth of their own sinfulness, their own unwillingness. It is the unwillingness of sinful people to come to the Lord. That's what keeps people away. They don't *want* to come. They don't want what the Lord offers.

You?

God's Honor

"I do not receive glory from people. But I know that you do not have the love of God within you. I have come in my Father's name, and you do not receive me. If another comes in his own name, you will receive him. How can you believe, when you receive glory from one another and do not seek the glory that comes from the only God?" —John 5:41-44

As Jesus concluded His defense of His divine mission, we should begin to see why the Jews had such a strong reaction to Him. We must be very careful here because we too can easily fall into the same reaction, with one significant difference. The modern reaction within the church is not so much against Jesus. Why not? Because Jesus has been redefined to suit the modern understanding—all loving, meek and mild. We have domesticated Jesus!

Today the reaction against the historical and biblical Jesus is so common that action is taken against those who preach and teach the traditional, historical view of the Lord because it is different from the modern redefinition. The current understanding is Jesus, meek and mild, ever loving, never confronting, always accepting people just as they are. It is a purely positive Jesus, nothing negative is allowed.

In contrast, the Scriptural view of Jesus, who confronts and admonishes the sinfulness of humanity, runs counter to the contemporary redefinition of Jesus. Over the centuries the Jews have been hated because of their hard-heartedness in their reaction against

Jesus. Antisemitism has resulted in the Christian community because of this understanding. But before we accuse the ancient Jews of being hard-hearted we must look at ourselves as we face the preaching of Christ crucified and risen.

Paul said in 1 Corinthians 1:23

> "we preach Christ crucified, to the Jews a stumbling block and to the Greeks foolishness."

According to Paul we have three options regarding the preaching of Christ crucified. We can stumble on it, see it as negative and as a problem. We can ignore it, dismiss it as foolishness. Or we can accept it in humility, believe it.

Don't Want It

This concluding section of Jesus' address to the Jews shows why so many souls are lost in this perishing world. Jesus held nothing back, but revealed the truth, the depravity, of the human heart. He wasn't concerned about appearing nice. Nor was He trying to be hurtful either. He simply told the truth from God's point of view. "You are not willing" He said in verse 40. Not for the lack of ability, nor because of the greatness of human sin, but for the lack of desire. As James (4:2) said, "you do not have because you do not ask." People do not have real faith because they don't really want it. It would change their lives too much. How would your life change if you were as faithful as Paul, or James, or John, etc.?

Most people think that their sins keep them from salvation. Even among professing Christians we find that people can talk about grace and forgiveness when asked, but there is a failure of genuine personal application. People want to qualify God's forgiveness, to think that it applies only to certain categories of sin—great sin, awful sin, but not to *their* sin. People think that their particular sins are just too grievous on the one hand or just too insignificant on the other, to receive God's forgiveness.

Others apply God's forgiveness in a mechanical way, like Catholics who go to confession, but keep sinning the same sins over and over, believing that confession justifies or absolves their continuing in sin. But in spite of all the fuss about sin, it is not sin that keeps people from salvation. It is their own unwillingness to be saved. It is the failure to submit to God's way of salvation through Christ.

It is common for people today to insist that God receive them just the way they are. But while God indeed loves people just the way they are, they cannot be received into God's presence just as they are because they are full of pride, deceit, and unforgiven sin. People must first be justified, cleansed. They must repent and be converted. They must be changed and covered—protected—by the Blood of Christ before God can receive them. And while that initial change requires nothing from the human side because it is entirely the work of the Holy Spirit, it does result in submission to Christ. Once beyond that initial justification, which is but a moment in time, it flowers into love and service to Christ producing the fruit of the Spirit. It requires no initial work, but it produces the hard work of faithfulness.

Jesus accused the Jews—and all unfaithful people—of four sins: 1) They do not truly love God (John 5:37). 2) They lack the will to submit to Jesus (John 5:40). 3) They seek the praise of men above the praise of God (John 5:43). 4) They lack real faith, practical belief in the Bible (John 5:46). We have already examined points one and two. We now turn to point three: the faithless prefer the praise of men more than the praise of God.

The Praise of Men

The contemporary understanding of this relates to political correctness, the craze to keep from offending others. The biblical principle that should be operative here is that there should be no offense but the Cross of Christ, which means that Christians should keep from all offensive words and behaviors, making every effort not to offend anyone. This principle is in step with modern political correctness.

Yet, Christians must also be willing and able to defend the cross of Christ from offense by others. Contemporary Christians are afraid of offending others, yet they think nothing of offending the Lord or of letting others offend the Lord. It seems that contemporary political correctness protects everyone except the Lord, everyone except Christians.

God is offended by the ban on school prayer, and by the ban on the public display of Christian symbols in public places. He is offended by art that portrays the cross in a bottle of urine. He is offended by the foul language of the street and the media. He is offended by sex and violence on television—and elsewhere. He is offended by a church that celebrates homosexuality as a God-given gift. He is offended when preachers fail to preach the gospel, and preach innocuous stories and a domesticated Savior in the place of repentance and salvation.

The modern church is offensive to God because it seeks to satisfy itself rather than God. The church caters to its own desires and definitions of success and growth. Modern churches will do anything to increase their membership. They go through every contortion imaginable to keep people comfortable in the face of a holy God. But all of Scripture mitigates against personal comfort before God. We cannot be comfortable before God because we are sinners.

To maintain our comfort we must deal with this issue of sin, one way or another. And it can be dealt with in one of only two possible ways. Sin is either accepted as a reality or denied. The reality of human sinfulness can only be understood as either true or false. Or so I thought! Modern theologians have found a third alternative. It is a mixed alternative, a mixed belief, neither true nor false, neither hot, nor cold.

Sin is acknowledged to be real, but is ignored as a foundational doctrine of theology. People acknowledge the reality of sin with their lips, but deny it in their hearts by thinking that they (or their wives, husbands, children, grandchildren, etc.) are basically good people. The modern church wants to have it both ways. So they confess sin in their liturgies, yet preach the goodness of their own loved ones.

And people like to hear that they are basically good. It is a popular teaching. It has brought new "success" to many churches over the past fifty years. The more successful it becomes, the more people want to hear it. And the more that people want to hear it, the more the church seeks the praise of men above the praise of God. And the more pressure there is upon preachers and teachers to minimize the doctrine of sin, and eliminate what by contrast seems to be so negative. People want to hear the positive aspects of the gospel, and nothing but the positive. So much so that anything resembling negativity is met with hostility and complaint. People turn off their hearing, and refuse to understand it.

The Context

There is much that is positive about the gospel. It is in fact primarily good news for all the world. But it is only good news in the light of God's Law. It is not good news by itself. It is not good news apart from the Old Testament. It is not good news apart from the conviction of sin and repentance. It is not good news apart from the desire to submit to God's Law. It is only good news when it is laid upon the proper foundation as in historic, biblical Christianity.

The Old Testament foundation takes into consideration the reality of human sin. Human history, the story of God's salvation, demonstrates the reality and tenacity of sin. But this foundational fact is denied by modern psychology and the academic, psychological worldview. Psychology understands people to be basically good. To explain human pain and deficiency they say that people have been psychologically damaged or emotionally injured because of some personal trauma during childhood (or since). Rather than sinful people dependent upon Jesus for salvation, we have victims of various circumstances dependent upon psychologists for curative treatment.

The psychological remedy for the emotional pain people experience is the recovery of their natural goodness. They believe that the recovery of basic human goodness will relieve emotional pain and stress. But it doesn't, and hasn't. This false understanding, rather than curing emotional pain and distress has aggravated it. And by aggravating it, it has also created an additional stumbling block to the gospel. That stumbling block is the belief in the natural goodness of humanity. The problem with this solution is that good people don't need Jesus!

To rescue the gospel from the grip of this false teaching, we must rediscover the reality of human sin. Sin must be seen for what it is. Unfortunately, that is perceived as negative by many people, and therefore it is dismissed out of hand, without further consideration. Consequently, the good news of the gospel has fallen by the wayside. Indeed, it has been thrown into the ditch, and devoured by well-meaning, but falsely informed birds—false because of their denial of the biblical context of the gospel.

This is the reality in which we live. People no longer honor the gospel. People no longer honor the Lord. As Jesus said in verse 42, the Jews had not the love of God in them. As Jesus accused the Jews, so He accuses the contemporary world. This is Jesus preaching to the Jews—and to us! He is preaching to everyone who does not have the love of God in their hearts.

In our day all sorts of preachers and preaching are entertained. Every manner of thought is preached as if it were the gospel of Christ. Listen to the radio, watch television preachers and you will see why there is such confusion about the gospel in our day. All sorts of garbage is thrown out to God's sheep. The sheep are left to defend for themselves, to determine what will nourish them and what will harm them.

The difficulty, of course, is that sheep cannot do that. Sheep feed indiscriminately. Extending the analogy to the human condition Christ's sheep feed on empty calories and all manner of chemical additives along with the rotting remains of God's truth, leftovers from a bygone era. After a while God's sheep believe that garbage is food, and are content to have whatever they can get, even if it gives them a belly ache.

How can God's truth be heard in the midst of so many contradicting voices? In such a situation it is tempting to believe that truth is relative, as we are taught in school. Relativity provides an easy way out of the dilemma. Most people have already succumbed to this temptation. It's an easy solution because if truth is relative, it doesn't matter what is preached. Truth itself is understood to be a matter of personal preference. If I like something, its true for me. If not, it isn't.

So, do I think that I have a corner on God's truth? Ha! I have consumed so much garbage myself that it is a wonder that I'm not dead already. But for the grace of God I would be. By the grace of God I have continued to seek the Lord (in the face of unbelievable garbage—only my wife really knows the full extent of it). But by the grace of God I now feed more discriminately. In spite of my wandering and incredible stupidity, the Lord has brought me home. And the sad truth is that my case is not unusual, but quite ordinary.

Seeing Beyond Our Expectations

In response I am constrained to preach upon the discrimination that the Lord has given me. I must point out as best I can what truly feeds the soul and what doesn't. My concern is the well-being of God's people, the well-being of my wife and children.

Pulpit & Pew

In this regard the pulpit is only for the preaching of God's Word. Nothing else should pass from the pulpit—not moralistic stories and current events, only God's Word. Preachers are called to preach God's Word, to preach Christ, crucified and risen. That is the purpose of the pulpit. That's the preacher's responsibility. God's Word needs to be preached all the more today because it is being drowned out by worldliness, inside and outside of the church.

And yet God's Word cannot become manifest simply by preaching. It must also be heard. The message must be received. God's Word also needs, not to be simply tolerated, but actually heard, received, believed. And the pews are for the hearing of it. When you sit in a pew, that is your responsibility. You need to hear it aright yourself, and then help others hear it aright. And to do that you must know it rightly.

These corresponding responsibilities of pulpit and pew are great responsibilities given by the Lord. Both are given by grace, both involve the hard work of faithfulness. They work together or they don't work at all. Caring for God's Word in this way is a matter of God's honor and God's glory. When it all works together and moves God's purpose forward in this sin-soaked world, it is truly a miracle. Praise be to God!

The Accuser

"How can you believe, when you receive glory from one another and do not seek the glory that comes from the only God? Do not think that I will accuse you to the Father. There is one who accuses you: Moses, on whom you have set your hope. For if you believed Moses, you would believe me; for he wrote of me. But if you do not believe his writings, how will you believe my words?" —John 5:44-47

When honor is accorded to someone, that person is held in high esteem and veneration. The one honored is also trusted. Their counsel is valued. Their perspective is appreciated. Their advice is heeded. There is an element of obedience that attaches to such honor. To honor advice is to heed it. Honor is much more than trust and obedience, of course, but it must include them or it is not honor.

Jesus says two things in verse 44. First, we must honor God, and second, we must seek the honor that comes from God. That is, we must desire to receive God's honor, to be able to stand at the judgment bench and know that God will say, "Well done, good and faithful servant" (Matthew 25:21). Such a servant is honored by the Lord. To be such a servant must be the desire of God's faithful people. If we want God to honor us, then we must be in His good graces, so to speak.

We must also realize that being a faithful servant of the Lord will gain the honor of none but God and those who honor Him. Friends and neighbors who don't honor God will find God's servants to be foolish at best. Service to the Lord will irritate worldly relationships because it will show others to be selfish and full of sin by comparison. A polished piece of brass near an unpolished piece will reveal the filth of the unpolished piece without doing anything to it.

Textual Confusion

Unfortunately, there is an added confusion for contemporary Bible readers. The AV reads, "and seek not the honor that cometh from God only" (v. 44). Whereas the NKJV reads, "and do not seek the honor that comes from the only God." The AV conveys the meaning that the only source of this honor is God. Whereas the NKJV suggests that while such honor must come from the only real God, it may also come from other sources. The only real God being the God who is present everywhere.

The correct reading from an historical standpoint must be the AV because it does not call into question the foundational doctrine of the Protestant Reformation—faith alone in Christ alone through Scripture alone. The difference between them is that the word *only* in the AV describes the source of the honor, where the word *only* in the NKJV describes the character of God. While both readings are technically correct, the AV relates to the context of the verse, while the NKJV introduces a subject not under consideration in these verses.

The purpose of God's Old Testament law was to demonstrate the moral failure of the Jews to conform to God's law. The failure extends to all of humanity. The law could not be fulfilled because of man's sin and depravity. God didn't goof up. The purpose of the law was not the fulfillment of the law, but the revealing of sin. The light of the law reveals the presence of sin. God knew all along that the law could not be fulfilled by sinful people. How can what is sinful be sinless?

Christ's Purpose

Then, when the time was right God sent His Son to fulfill the law, to be a sinless sacrifice and provide God's righteousness as a gift through faith. Jesus Christ lived a sinless life and fulfilled God's law.

It was not Jesus' purpose to reveal human sinfulness—the law already does that. Christ's purpose was to reveal God's grace, given for human salvation through the righteousness of Christ. Consequently, Jesus said that He would not go before God to accuse the Jews of faithlessness. He didn't need to do that because the law of Moses had already done that.

But that was not the way the Jews saw it. They believed that they were indeed fulfilling the law through the maintenance of the various traditions, sacrifices, rules of behavior, etc. They thought that was all God wanted. So they were satisfied with their adherence to the law as defined by the Pharises. They thought they were doing all that God required. They misunderstood the prophets in this, but nonetheless they believed it.

In fact, without God's further revelation of grace through Christ, it was quite natural for the Jews to believe as they did. They saw nothing beyond the fulfillment of the law of Moses. For them, that was the height of faithfulness. It was only through the revelation of grace through Christ that the law could be understood to have been a mere half-way measure for an infant church. Only with the revelation of grace through Christ could the law be seen for what it always was.

But in order to see this, one must first see the truth of God's revelation of grace through Christ. Apart from Christ, engagement of the law was understood to be the highest end of human living. Only by the grace of faith in Christ was the law put into its proper perspective. In essence, Jesus said to the Jews, *If you believe the presuppositions of Moses, then you should believe the Mosaic conclusion as well*—that conclusion being Himself, God's Messiah. The Old Testament predicted the coming of Messiah, the One who would put the law and the prophets in proper perspective. That was the ancient Old Testament prediction. So it should have been no surprise that the Messiah had come. But it was so unexpected that it was rejected.

Training

Moses and the prophets had predicted His coming. So, if they had believed Moses and the prophets rightly, they should surely have believed in the reality of the promised Messiah. But as the case of the

Jews proves, the belief of faith is not a matter of simply deciding to believe. The Jews could not reverse the cultural indoctrination of many centuries by a simple decision to believe. Something more was required to bring about changed hearts and minds.

Imagine a little boy who decides that when he grows up he wants to be a fireman. He has decided to be a fireman, but that decision has not made him a fireman. The possibility of his becoming a fireman is still a long way off. In spite of his decision, the reality of his situation is that he is still a little boy. He has much work to do before he can be a fireman. He has school and firemen training to complete.

But even completing the training required of firemen will not itself make him a fireman. It is possible to take all the required training and still not be a fireman. Training alone does not make a fireman. You can't be a fireman without it, but more than training is required. There are also exams to pass. Simply completing the training doesn't guarantee passing the exams. But even when the exams have been passed, the boy—now older and wiser—will still not actually be a fireman. To be a fireman, he must be hired by a fire company—and that decision is not his to make.

Consider two equal applicants applying for one fireman's job. One gets the job and one doesn't. Both decided to be firemen. Both trained for it and passed the tests with equal scores. Both are the same age and health. But one gets the job and one doesn't. What is the difference? The difference is that the final decision does not belong to the person who wants the job. The final decision rests with the employer, not the employee.

The analogy is less than perfect when applied to God's grace, but the point is that the salvation decision is God's, not ours. Of course our decision plays a key role in the process, but it is not the decisive role. God decided to offer the grace of salvation through faith in Jesus Christ. The gift of salvation was entirely God's doing, freely given yet entirely of God. It was God's idea, just like the hiring of the fireman must be the idea of the employer.

The employer has an idea in his mind of the kind of fireman that he will hire. He must have certain qualifications, training, and experience, etc. So, the boy who is serious about being a fireman must know what the future employer has in mind, and then conform his life to the fire chief's understanding of what it takes to be a fireman—not his own idea, but the boss's idea. If he expects to actually land a job he must know what is expected of him by the person who has the authority to actually hire him.

Knowledge

So it is with Christians. We must know what God has in mind regarding the kind of people He will save. The job description of a Christian was written by God, and we must know what is expected. The decision lies with the firechief, not the boy—and by analogy, with God, not with us—although we must willingly agree with God. Certainly, the boy has decisions to make, as do we. But the point is that none of his decisions can guarantee the job. Salvation is God's idea, and it will be accomplished according to God's plan, not ours. Applied to Christianity the analogy fails in as much as it suggests that we can satisfy God's expectations through our own efforts. The truth is that we cannot. But the truth is also that God sent His Holy Spirit to regenerate His people in order to add His own strength to theirs to insure their salvation.

In spite of our inability to satisfy God's law, Jesus did not come to point His finger at people and accuse them of moral failure, no matter how great their sin. Rather, Jesus came to point His finger toward God, and to provide the way of salvation. We in turn are to point people to God's Word.

It does no good for one person to accuse another of moral failure. The one being accused will simply find some way to dismiss or devalue the accusation or the accuser. The accuser will be dismissed as being one of those horrible fundamentalists, or a religious extremist, or crazy, or whatever. But the accusation will not penetrate the defense of the ego. Direct accusation won't usually work.

Penetration

Only the Holy Spirit can penetrate the defenses of the ego. Only the Holy Spirit can convict someone of sin. We must allow the Holy Spirit to make whatever accusations are necessary. He knows the heart, we don't. The conviction of sin cannot come from without. It cannot be imposed upon people. Rather, it must come from within a person. Successful conviction works to undermine egoic defenses from within. Accusation from without usually hardens the ego's defenses. Real conviction comes only when the Holy Spirit uses a person's own conscience to convict him of sin. The most successful accuser is a person's own conscience.

That means that a person's conscience must be sensitized to God's Word and God's values. By learning God's Word and adopting God's values a person comes to see his own failings through the power of the Holy Spirit. A person's own conscience then begins to accuse the person of transgression against God's law. And in this way does the accusation become effective, able to prick the heart, to convince and convict the person of sin. Only by knowing God's punishment for sin can people come to realize how important salvation really is.

So, people must know about God's punishment for sin. People must understand the seriousness of sin. The only way to effectively teach these things is to teach the Bible, the whole Bible, warts and all.

Each generation and each individual must come to an understanding of the significance of sin and salvation for themselves—not *by* themselves, but *for* themselves. Each generation and each individual must be convicted anew. Each generation and each individual must be saved anew. While the sins of the fathers may effect the children for generations to come, the salvation of the parents does not guarantee the salvation of the children.

Our job as Christians is to point to God's Word. Always and in everything we must lift up God's Word, proclaim it abroad, and teach it to our families and friends—particularly to our own children. We are all sinners and as sinners we are on equal ground before God. Our most righteous acts are but filthy rags before God (Isaiah 64:6). We are all guilty of sin and deserving of death.

We must point to God's Word because as we do that we will not only convict others of God's grace and mercy, but we will also be convicted of our own sin. And the good news of God's grace is that God only saves sinners—not simply forgiven sinners, but accused and convicted sinners. Unaccused sinners will remain unconvicted.

Unconvicted sinners cannot receive forgiveness. Only accused and convicted sinners can receive mercy. And conviction comes through the miraculous activity of the Holy Spirit in the lives of individuals. Thus, the conviction of sin is a miracle. And all who receive the conviction of sin by the Holy Spirit will also receive God's forgiving grace.

How can I be so sure of this? Because once the Holy Spirit touches a heart with the conviction of sin, that heart is under the influence of the Holy Spirit. That's the only way that conviction of sin can effectually happen. Therefore, that heart, if the conviction be genuine, cannot help but follow the Holy Spirit to the grace of God in Christ Jesus. Once conviction of sin penetrates a heart, all other resistance is futile. God will have His way.

Food For The Hungry

The Test

"After this Jesus went away to the other side of the Sea of Galilee, which is the Sea of Tiberias. And a large crowd was following him, because they saw the signs that he was doing on the sick. Jesus went up on the mountain, and there he sat down with his disciples. Now the Passover, the feast of the Jews, was at hand. Lifting up his eyes, then, and seeing that a large crowd was coming toward him, Jesus said to Philip, 'Where are we to buy bread, so that these people may eat?' He said this to test him, for he himself knew what he would do. Philip answered him, 'Two hundred denarii would not buy enough bread for each of them to get a little.' —John 6:1-7

It is interesting to note that John recorded no response to Jesus' long speech to the Jews. Jesus just finished issuing a very strong challenge, which has been covered in the last few chapters of this book, and which was sure to elicit a strong reaction. You may have been challenged yourself as you felt the impact of Jesus' accusation against a mechanical and lifeless faith, like the faith of the Pharisees. Jesus' words would have deeply disturbed the Jews who heard Him. Yet, no response is recorded. I suspect John left it that way so that future readers could be confronted with their own response to Jesus' challenge.

When Jesus finished His monologue he returned to Galilee, probably for some rest and relaxation. Or perhaps he went to escape some trouble that may have developed among the Jews to whom He had been speaking. Scripture doesn't say why He went, only that He went by way of the Sea of Galilee near Tiberias.

If He had gone for rest and relaxation, He was out of luck because "a great multitude followed Him" (v. 2). Apparently He had created quite a stir. His miracles and His unrelenting challenge to the Jewish establishment that was so bound by its own traditions undoubtedly attracted attention. We know it did because even the Pharisees noticed. Word was out that Jesus may have been some kind of prophet. And now the rumors about Him had drawn a crowd.

The masses who followed Him at this point probably weren't responding to any high spiritual principles or religious commitment. More than likely, most of the crowd followed Jesus because of a vague curiosity about miracles and prophets, and for the love of excitement and the hope of throwing off the yoke of Rome. Talking as He did, He could likely draw the ire of the Sanhedrin. Perhaps a fight was brewing. That will draw a crowd every time.

Crowds then were much like crowds today. Crowds are drawn by curiosity and the lure of excitement. Seldom are crowds motivated by religious principles. Generally those with religious principles stay away from crowds. The mentality of the crowd is usually pretty low. Crowds are subject to gross morality and emotional inflammation. When a mob gathers anything can happen. In a crowd principles tend to flow to the lowest common denominator.

Verse 2 tells us that the crowd followed him "because they saw His signs which He performed on those who were diseased," (v. 2—*astheneō*). The Greek word indicates the same sickness that had afflicted the man at the Bethesda pool. A*stheneō,* was a generic term that covered a lot of different illnesses that always resulted in a general weakness and lethargy. It was a condition dominated by lethargy, which would include spiritual apathy. John suggests here that Jesus had healed others from this affliction, not just the Bethesda man. John suggests not only that others were healed, but that a lot of people suffered from this illness which Jesus cured. If I may extrapolate, when a nation's religion is sick, a lot of people suffer from apathy.

This story of the feeding of the five thousand is of particular significance because it is the only miracle story recorded in all four Gospels. For this reason alone we must accord it particular attention.

We must try to discover why it is so important. We also note again that John's gospel was the last to be written, and it appears to have been written as a correction of sorts to the others.

At some point in the story Jesus went ashore and set up camp on a nearby mountain. His camp would not have been very high up the mountain because it overlooked a large grassy field where the multitude gathered, and from where Jesus spoke to them. A large multitude would not have climbed very high.

He went up the mountain with "His disciples" (v. 3). Among His disciples were, or course, the twelve who had been chosen and set apart by Jesus. But no doubt there were others "who (had) professed themselves His disciples."[1] In the crowd were many self-professed Christians who were not really believers. We know this from verse 66 of this same chapter, where we learn that when Jesus moved from performing miracles to teaching doctrine, "many of His disciples went back and walked with Him no more." We'll get to that story later, but we now need to see that the seeds of shallow belief were already here in the gathering crowd.

In verse 4 we learn that it was Passover again. During the last Passover Jesus had chased the money-changers from the Temple (John 2). So, a year had passed between then and now. But we also know, because Passover was near, that there were a lot of people on the roads, traveling to Jerusalem for the holidays. This fact likely accounts for the crowd that Jesus had drawn. For many travelers to stop and see Jesus would have been an attractive diversion on their trip to Jerusalem. Many of them would have remembered Jesus from the previous Passover, and would have thought it worth the detour to see what was going on at Tiberias.

Needless to say, travelers carry provisions for their journey. It would be foolish for them not to do so, and for us not to know so. We will return to this observation shortly.

Jesus normally attended Passover, but that year He missed it. By missing Passover Jesus taught that outward ordinances and ceremonies do not need to be blindly and mechanically followed. That was His argument against the Pharisees. We all know that there are

---

1 Ryle, p. 331.

times when extenuating circumstances prohibit one's presence at religious ceremonies.

> "Grace, and repentance, and faith are absolutely needful to salvation. Sacraments and ordinances are not."[2]

As the crowd gathered Jesus "lifted up His eyes." That is an unusual expression. The Greek word *epairo*, translated "lifted up," is used nineteen times in the New Testament. It is used for lifting up one's head, hands, eyes, and voice in response to the divine presence. Here it is used as a loftier looking than plain seeing. Here when Jesus "lifted up His eyes" He not only saw the crowd, but He was also aware of God's presence in the midst of the crowd. God's hand was upon the crowd. That's what Jesus saw. That's why He lifted up His eyes to them. God was about to minister to them or through them. Jesus lifted up His eyes and saw a miracle about to happen.

Notice that Jesus initiated the idea of feeding the crowd. That in itself should be an indication of His love and care for people. Before they even noticed that they were hungry, Jesus had already set into motion provision for their need. But from the outset we can see that Jesus had in mind more than simply providing food.

He set the situation up by asking Philip if he knew where to *buy* bread for such a large crowd. Philip would have known because Philip came from Galilee. He was on home turf. He would know where to find such a large quantity of bread, if indeed such a quantity was available anywhere in or around Tiberias.

Surely Jesus knew that there were no large bakeries in the area. In Matthew's version (14:15) Jesus' disciples called the area a "deserted place." It was out in the sticks. Not only was it a desolate area, but John went on to say that Jesus was testing Philip. Testing him for what? About what? The traditional answer is that Jesus was testing Philip's faith. Would Philip be able to simply trust Jesus to miraculously produce food?

There is no question that Jesus was testing Philip's faith. What is unclear is the nature of the test. What about Philip's faith was being tested? Philip had no reason to think that Jesus would miraculously produce bread. Jesus had never done anything like that before. There

---

2 Ibid.

is no reason for Philip to suggest such a miracle. And we all know that Jesus' disciples were not very quick on the uptake.

Was Jesus looking for blind faith? Or was He looking for something more specific? It wasn't just Philip who was being tested. The other disciples were listening in, and being tested as well—as are we.

If we believe that Jesus wants His disciples to simply have blind faith and trust without thinking about everything that He does, we will turn Jesus into a kind of magician who pulls bread from a magic hat. But Jesus wasn't a magician, nor did He want us to think of Him as a magician. Quite the opposite, superstition and magic were being destroyed by the advent of Christianity. Nor was it blind faith that Jesus was looking for. The Lord of the universe needs thinking disciples. Something else was going on. But what?

The question that Jesus asked wasn't about faith at all. It was about bread. It wasn't a theoretical question, but a practical one. Jesus asked a practical question about a practical matter.

Where will we find enough food to feed such a large crowd? You know this area, Phil. What do you think?

The issue that Jesus brought up was about the source of the resources needed to feed the crowd. Even if there had been a bakery nearby, no bakery of that day would have been able to provide for such a large crowd.

Thus, the issue that Jesus was testing Philip and the disciples about was the doctrine of God's providence. Did they believe in God's providence? Would they trust God for provision? Where would Philip turn to find food for God's people? The issue was not Philip's faith per se, but his trust in God's providence. Clearly the disciples were unable to care for such a large crowd from their own resources. The twelve or fifteen disciples (or forty with wives and children) couldn't have the provisions to feed five thousand. Surely Jesus knew this. What Jesus wanted to know was whether they would trust God to provide a practical solution to a real problem?

In a sense Jesus asked if it was possible to depend upon the current social and economic system to provide for the needs of the people. I'm not talking about some college understanding of economics as an abstract science. I'm talking about the everyday occurrence of buying and selling bread and eggs. Jesus asked Philip if he knew where to *buy* bread, not get it but *buy* it. Jesus asked if there was a market or a town near that could provide for their needs.

John said that Jesus did this on purpose. It was an intentional set up. Jesus was going to teach the disciples a lesson about God's economy. Could the market, and the economic system that supported it, be relied upon to meet their needs? Jesus asked if it was necessary to depend upon a market economy to feed God's people. Any miraculous understanding of this feeding must include the understanding that God's provision was outside of the ordinary economy of things.

Note also that Jesus didn't ask for yogurt and cheese. He asked specifically for bread (*artos*). *Artos* was a common but particular kind of wheat bread made in the form of an oblong or round cake, as thick as one's thumb, and as large as a plate or platter. It probably looked like thick pizza crust. Jesus called for a particular lunch menu, *artos*.

It was not Philip's lack of faith that led him to answer as he did. He was led by Jesus' question. He answered the question Jesus asked. But Jesus didn't ask him in order to get an answer—as if Jesus didn't know the answer already. Again, John said that Jesus asked him in order to test him.

In college I took a class called "Creativity and Problem Solving." It was an art class. It's a long story, and not worth much consideration. But it provides an example of Philip's situation. On the first day of class the teacher brought in about fifty cardboard boxes, and divided the class into two teams. "The team to make the highest stack of boxes wins," he instructed. That was it. That was the first problem, and we were to solve it.

The teams came up with various methods to stack boxes, but in the end the teacher won all by himself by stacking the boxes from the bottom up rather than from the top down. He picked up the stack of empty boxes and slid additional boxes into the stack from the bottom. His stack rose higher and higher. He didn't need ladders, or other people to boost him up. The lesson was that the solution to a problem is always limited by one's ability to see the various elements of the problem without preconceptions.

That was the kind of problem that Philip faced. It wasn't an abstract problem about his faith, but a practical problem about his trust. Jesus wanted to know if Philip and the disciples were bound by the current economic thinking of their world. That was the test. *Do we need to buy food?* Jesus asked.

Philip answered by calling attention to the fact that all the money they had, two hundred denari, could not buy enough bread to feed such a large crowd. We can assume two hundred denari to be a lot of money. The point was that they didn't have enough money to buy enough bread to feed that many people. And even if they did, there was no market in the area large enough to sell that much bread. Jesus asked an economic question about buying bread, and Philip gave an economic answer.

Jesus' question set up an impossible situation. They didn't have the resources to solve the problem. They could not depend upon the economy. Neither all the money they had, nor any available market inventory, could supply their needs.

What would they do? That was the test. How would they solve this problem? When their own resources were not enough, would they trust God to provide? What would they do when they were at the end of their own resources? The test was not about the faith of the disciples, but about trusting God's provision. Would God provide for the need of the hour? God always does.

The Source

"One of his disciples, Andrew, Simon Peter's brother, said to him, 'There is a boy here who has five barley loaves and two fish, but what are they for so many?' Jesus said, 'Have the people sit down.' Now there was much grass in the place. So the men sat down, about five thousand in number." —John 6:8-10

Here Jesus provided a test was for all of His disciples. At this point Andrew, Simon Peter's brother, got into the act, but again the test involved more than the Twelve. Matthew, Mark, Luke, and John all captured the essence of the test—the miracle—and preserved it for all generations of disciples. In reality, we are more than just watching Jesus test His disciples. We are also being tested right now as we watch. Our test is to see the real miracle.

The test has something to do with the feeding of the five thousand. In the last chapter we determined that miracles were more than a simple test of blind faith. Jesus was always interested in intelligent faith, not blind faith. Jesus wanted to see how much the disciples believed in God's providence. Would God provide what the disciples could not provide? Would the disciples see the supernatural providence of God?

There are many people today who trust in God's providence. I have heard stories of people who have committed themselves to Jesus Christ beyond their own resources. I'm not suggesting that you do such a thing, or that you don't. What you trust to God is between you and Jesus. I'm only telling a story.

The Baynes

The Bayne family consisted of a husband, wife, and three young children. Bob couldn't hold a job. He had back trouble and poor health. And Betty had three young children. Money was always tight. They patched together a very old car, and lived in a run-down, two-bedroom apartment in a poor part of town. But they loved the Lord, and they gave generously to the Lord—more generously than I thought they should.

One day when I visited them, they told me a story of how God's providence had sustained them that week. They were flat broke as usual. The cupboards were bare. Bob wasn't working and they had no prospect of any money coming in. They prayed daily for God's care. The day their rent was due a check came in the mail. Apparently there had been an accounting error from one of Bob's previous jobs. Bob had been underpaid, and the amount was almost exactly what they needed to pay the rent. Praise be to God!

The long and the short of it was that money appeared in their hour of need. It was God's providence at work. I could sight other examples, but more examples will be unnecessary for those who know about God's providence, and will not convince those who don't.

The principle of God's providence is not that God necessarily creates a supernatural miracle every time His people are in need. God could do that if He chose to, but generally that is not the way He works. God's providence usually works within the normal limitations of the natural world, and sometimes unexpectedly so. God prefers to use ordinary means whenever possible. The check did not materialize out of thin air, it came from within the natural order at an ordinary time of need under the influence of prayer.

God's providence normally comes out of the abundance of the blessings of the natural order, from blessings already bestowed, but unseen. God gives abundantly and He's been doing so for a long time. Prayer opens the portals of heaven and sensitizes God's people to the power of the Holy Spirit to find provision where there once was none, to see provision where it was previously unseen.

God's providence will not make you rich. If God blesses you with much, He will also show you much need among His people. God's providence is not for people to hoard. Mostly, God bestows the blessings of His provision by revealing resources that were previously overlooked or dismissed. John suggests that the feeding of the five thousand is such a case.

As we proceed, please note that we are reading Scripture literally.[3] This story of the feeding of the five thousand is not a parable, and not poetry. It is history. It is situated in a particular time—Passover, at a particular place—Tiberias. The people were real people. It is history. So, we will look carefully at exactly what Scripture says, and what it doesn't say. Let's look at the story again.

The Market

Jesus asked Philip if the disciples could buy *artos* for the crowd of five-thousand. *Artos* was a particular kind of whole wheat bread that resembled pizza crust. Philip immediately looked into the purse to see if they had enough money. They didn't. But even if they had, there was no place to buy it, no bakeries nearby.

Perhaps I'm making too much of the word *artos* here. Jesus could just as well have meant bread of any kind, or even food of any kind. So, let's be as generous as possible with our interpretation by taking Jesus to mean any kind of food. He was concerned about their hunger, though He had bread in mind. They had followed Him into the wilderness and He was concerned about their well-being. He knew that they could not live by bread alone (Matthew 4:4), so He was feeding them God's Word.

He asked Philip if the disciples could *buy* the crowd something to eat. Jesus used the word *buy*. Matthew and Mark recorded that Jesus wanted the people to *buy* food (*agorazo*, literally: *to go to the market*) for themselves (Matthew 14:15, Mark 6:36). So the idea was to *buy* food. Luke remembered Jesus to have said,

> "Send the multitude away, that they may go into the surrounding towns and country, and lodge and get provisions; for we are in a deserted place here" (Luke 9:12).

---

3 To take Scripture literally means to follow the exact words of the original, to use a word-for-word translation. That excludes nearly all Bible translations. The modern translations use the dynamic equivalence method of translation, which by definition is not literal. But even the King James Version does not follow the Greek word-for-word. A literal translation is more like *Young's Literal Translation of the Holy Bible*, Robert Young, Baker Book House, 1862 (reprinted), or *Green's Literal Translation*, Jay P. Green, Sr., Sovereign Grace Trust Fund, Lafayette, Indiana, 1995.

Luke used the Greek *heurisko*, which is translated as *find* ninety-eight percent of the time. Surely Jesus didn't mean for them to steal or borrow food. He could only have meant for them to *buy* food.

The point is that Jesus set up the test by suggesting that someone *purchase* food for the crowd. Jesus asked about a market or a town where food could be procured. The provision that they needed was beyond the immediate resources of those present—beyond the resources of the disciples. They were in the wilderness with five-thousand people, and Jesus wanted lunch.

Barley

In verse 8 Andrew took another look at their available resources. Here within the crowd was a young boy with five loaves and two small fish. Only John noticed what kind of loaves they were—barley. Not wheat, but barley. The boy had barley loaves. Is that significant? John thought it important enough to record. John mentioned the fact that the loaves were barley because he was trying to point out the real nature of the miracle. Only John mentioned the fact that Jesus was testing His disciples. Their test was to perceive the real miracle.

Farmers know about barley. The rest of us have to learn about it in books. My Bible dictionary says regarding barley,

> "Cereals and the art of converting them into bread were probably God's direct gift to man from the first."[4]

Bread, any kind of bread, is one of the original provisions given by God. But the dictionary goes on to say that barley was considered to be inferior to wheat. A measure of wheat was equivalent to three measures of barley (Revelation 6:6) at the market. John has given us this information for a reason. We must discover its significance.

Barley was mostly used for animal feed. People could eat it, but generally preferred not to. So, why was the boy carrying *barley* loaves? Could the barley have been animal feed? It could well be that the boy had been charged to care for the animals. Such a job would not be uncommon.

The boy also had two small fish. Such fish were staple around the Sea of Galilee. The fish were, no doubt, for his journey and not for

---

4 *Home Bible Study Dictionary*, A.R. Fausset, Kregel Publications, 1987, p. 77.

the animals. Dried fish traveled well and could be eaten or sold to other holiday travelers. The fish were undoubtedly the boy's provision for the trip.

We don't know if anyone else had any provisions with them. There is no mention of any such thing. But it is important to notice that Scripture is careful to tell us nothing about it. We don't know if they did, or if they didn't. Scripture simply doesn't say. What was John's reason for mentioning that the loaves were barley? How God provided the bread was not as important as the fact that it was God who provided it. It was not outside of ordinary providence, but it was outside of the Disciples' expectations.

Jesus immediately saw the potential. John said that He "lifted up His eyes" (v. 5) and saw God's hand among the people. Five loaves and two fish were enough to make the connection. "Make the people sit down," Jesus said (v. 10). Why did John mention the sitting down? What difference could that possibly make?

The Grass

Where did they sit? John pointed out the odd fact that "there was much grass in the place" (v. 10). Many commentators have been quick to note that God was so very kind to have even provided a nice grassy meadow for a picnic, as if the grass simply provided a pleasant place to sit. Why would John bother to mention grass in the context of this story? Because God provided it for a reason. Could it be that the animals could graze on the grass, which would free up barley, that was intended for the animals, for the people. And all God's creatures would be fed. Surely travelers would be concerned about the well-being of their animals on a trip in the wilderness. Perhaps the miracle was God's provision of grass for the animals, which would free up the barley for the people.

It's just speculation, but it points us to a more important miracle in the story. John didn't want us to confuse the fact that people brought food with them with the greater miracle that was wrought. Again, John's was the last gospel to be written. In writing last he may have been clarifying a point of confusion that had arisen about this particular miracle. John seems to insinuate that there was more involved than the supernatural materialization of bread out of thin air. John provided enough additional information to sustain an alternative understanding, and to point to a greater miracle.

The greater miracle was that God has always provided for His people—always has and always will. John looked beyond the instantaneous satisfaction of the material needs of the crowd, beyond the momentary gratification of the body, while at the same time faithfully reporting that the material needs of the people were indeed satisfied.

Outside The Box

Rather, John points out that the miracle was the fact that God's provision appeared unexpectedly from an unforeseen source. Did God miraculously create a field of grass? Yep. It was probably a while back, but it was God's creation—and it was a miracle. What was already there—both barley and grass—were both gifts from God and sufficient for the needs of God's people. The miracle wasn't simply the appearance of food out of thin air. Rather, the miracle was to be found in the source and manner of its appearing. That is, from God with prayer.

The same thing happened with the Bayne family. There was no magic involved. The gospel has always been opposed to magic. Rather, the miracle was wrought by prayer and trust in God's providence. Jesus modeled it by praying and trusting God Himself. Jesus modeled it in everything. Jesus always prayed and trusted God, no matter what the outcome. God always provided, even in Jesus' death.

Is it any less of a miracle if bread didn't materialize out of thin air? Not a bit. In fact, it reveals an even greater miracle—greater because it opens up God's providence to all His people for all time. Not by way of magic, but by simple prayer and the expectation of a movement of the Holy Spirit—trusting that God will provide by showing us what is already there. God's providence is as available to us today as it was to those five thousand people on the grassy field in the hills of Galilee. God's provision is usually a matter of seeing what God has already provided, seeing with new eyes.

If it had simply been a miraculous materialization of bread, the miracle would have been a one time event, over and done with that day. But because it involved the miracle of seeing God's providence within the natural realm, it demonstrates the assurance of God's providence for all time. If God could do it like that out in the wilderness, God can do it anywhere. Jesus opened up the eyes of His people to see the stores of God's providence—not just on that one occasion, but forevermore! That's the special importance of this miracle.

Of course, God could have materialized bread out of thin air. Nothing is impossible for God (Jeremiah 32:17). Such a thing would be easy for God. God could have done such a thing. But Scripture doesn't say that He did it that way. It doesn't say He didn't, either. Jesus could have made bread from stones. But He didn't.

Remember when Jesus was tempted in the desert? Satan said, "If You are the Son of God, command that these stones become bread" (Matthew 4:3). Jesus could have done it, no question. But He didn't. Rather, He answered and said,

> "It is written, 'Man shall not live by bread alone, but by every word that proceeds from the mouth of God'" (Matthew 4:4).

He told Satan that God's Word is infinitely more important than bread. God's most important provision is His Word. The provision contained in God's Word is infinitely more important than the feeding of five-thousand hungry people. Which is the greater miracle? To provide lunch for five-thousand? Or to provide salvation for all God's people? To give a man lunch, or to teach him to see God's provision with new eyes, so that he can find his own lunch in any environment? How is salvation provided in this story? Verse 14 reads,

> "Then those men, who had seen the sign that Jesus did, said, 'This is truly the Prophet who is to come into the world.'"

We know that Jesus was more than a prophet. In that regard those men were wrong. But from that day forward they accorded Jesus the highest status they could imagine: God's prophet for the hour. We know Him as God's Messiah. They would soon know Him in the same way.

The application of God's providence is timely in today's world of economic trouble, like it was for the Baynes. Pray, and trust God to provide. But don't close your eyes, hoping for provision to suddenly materialize out of thin air. Rather, keep your eyes open. Look for the hand of God to be already moving within the limitations of your situation. Look for the provision that is already there. Pray, and trust God to provide.

The Remainder

"Jesus then took the loaves, and when he had given thanks, he distributed them to those who were seated. So also the fish, as much as they wanted. And when they had eaten their fill, he told his disciples, 'Gather up the leftover fragments, that nothing may be lost.' So they gathered them up and filled twelve baskets with fragments from the five barley loaves left by those who had eaten. When the people saw the sign that he had done, they said, 'This is indeed the Prophet who is to come into the world!'

—John 6:11-14

The case has now been made that Jesus wrought two miracles, or perhaps two aspects of a single miracle, with the feeding of the five thousand. There was 1) the immediate miracle of the manifestation of additional food for the crowd, and 2) the greater miracle of the opening of God's providential stores to His people for all time by teaching His people how to see God's providence.

We have thus far considered three explanations of the immediate miracle of the feeding of the five thousand. The first explanation was the miraculous manifestation of bread (*artos*) where none had previously been. This is the traditional interpretation suggested in the other three Gospels. The second was the miracle of God's provision in creation itself. In this instance, providing grass for the animals, which freed up the barley for the people. And third was the provision of barley. Because John was the only Evangelist who mentioned barley, this aspect of the miracle is unique to him.

Thus far we have three possible manifestations of God's miraculous providence: bread, grass for the animals, and barley loaves. Each of these are natural elements that God provides daily for the world. There are also two categories of explanations regarding God's miraculous providence in the case before us: 1) the natural explanations and 2) the supernatural explanations.

THE EXPLANATIONS

The natural explanations attempt to account for the miracle in a wholly naturalistic way. The natural explanation of the appearance of additional bread is that the crowd already had bread with them and simply shared it among themselves. While this explanation has been generally rejected by the church, it does reveal the miracle of generosity, cooperation, and unity among God's people. Yet, it provides an unsatisfactory explanation because it falls short of the entire biblical account.

The supernatural explanation is that God produced bread out of thin air. God's people are then asked to believe this miraculous manifestation as a matter of blind faith—blind because to my knowledge no one since has ever witnessed such a thing. Such a miracle is certainly possible for God, but it raises issues about magic and blind faith that are out of character for God. If Jesus wouldn't produce bread from stones for Satan, why would He produce magical bread for this crowd?

The natural explanation of the grass is that God provided it as a natural part of creation and set the context of the miracle in the vicinity of the grassy meadow. The grass then provided food for the animals, freeing up the animal feed (barley) for the people so that all of God's creatures were then providentially fed, with plenty left over.

Here the miracle involved a rethinking and reallocation of available, natural resources. This explanation reveals the miracle of creation, which demonstrates the practical reality in which God's providence continues to function. This is the way we experience God's providence today. But again, such an explanation proves unsatisfactory for many people because it doesn't involve a breach of the natural order. It seems much too ordinary to be miraculous. It avails itself of no need for any supernatural explanation because nothing supernatural occurred. Or did it? Here the miracle involves seeing with new eyes, and new eyes are miraculous.

The third possibility, John's barley loaves, has both a natural and a supernatural explanation. The natural explanation suggests that the crowd carried provision for their animals, but were without sufficient provision for the massive crowd. They had barley, but not enough wheat bread to go around.

Bringing barley loaves with them on their journey would have had a multiple purpose. Such loaves could feed the animals or, in case of emergency, they could eat them themselves, or they could be sold if they needed something else. Barley could have served as an emergency provision. The introduction of the grass, then, would have been the immediate gift of God's provision in the miracle. Here the miracle would be a matter of God's timing, of putting them there at that time, and not simply His immediate production of anything. The miracle here was the *seeing* of His provision where none was seen before. The miracle was what we might call *new eyes*.

John, while introducing the necessary information to sustain such a naturalistic explanation, was not content with a natural explanation. In verses 12 and 13 he showed that by the command of Jesus, the barley loaves had been miraculously multiplied. Thus, reopening the door to the traditional supernatural explanation of bread from thin air. Or did he? Animals are large and eat more than people do. So, if there had been a lot of animals, and people carrying provision for them, we could expect leftovers because the animals didn't need it.

God could certainly create *ex niliho*. God had done it before. When Elijah was fed by the ravens, he begged bread from a widow. But the widow said that she had barely a handful of flour and was nearly out of oil as well. Elijah instructed her, and when she obeyed his instructions her flour and oil did not run out. There was enough for her and her son, and Elijah (1 Kings 17:12-16). There were many such miracles in the Old Testament. Clearly, God could have produced any miracle He wanted.

But John was very specific in his reintroduction of the supernatural aspect of the miracle when he mentioned the leftovers. John specified that the twelve baskets of fragments were "the fragments of *the (same) five barley loaves*" (v. 13—emphasis added). By mentioning barley he emphasized the idea that it had been animal feed.

Economy

Note that none of the explanations—natural or supernatural—regarding the wheat bread, the barley loaves, or the grass have any effect upon the greater miracle of God's ongoing providential care. None of it has anything to do with us today. The point of the miracle was that the disciples did not need to rely upon their local economy or marketplace to provide for God's people.[5] Rather, God's people could—and indeed, we *must*—rely upon God's economy. God had provided all that was needed, and did so apart from the management of the crowd by the disciples.

The test here was for the disciples to *see* and tap into the miracle of God's economy, the economy that existed outside of the ordinary marketplace, beyond their assumptions and expectations. This miracle involved the spirit of sharing that did not require ordinary marketplace mechanisms. And while you might think that sharing is hardly a miracle, I encourage you to look around the world today and think again. These people were in the desert without sufficient food, and cut off from the marketplace. Sure, it's not as "big" a miracle as creating bread from nothing, but it is much more real. And it is available to all. And such sharing could still feed the world today!

The explanations differ as to how God provided, whether through His natural creation or by supernatural intervention. But how God provided is the concern of God alone. The fact of the provision is to be the object of trust by the people of God. John's point was that the greater miracle stood, no matter what kind of explanation was given for the feeding of the crowd. The fact that God provided is the special importance of this miracle.

John did not completely obscure the supernatural aspect of this miracle because God had manifested many supernatural miracles in history and, therefore, He could have done so again. The supernatural explanation must not be eliminated because it was a real factor in the situation. John honored the fact that nothing is impossible for

---

5   The word *economy* is used here in the sense of a marketplace for the exchange of goods and services.

God. Both the manufacture of bread from thin air and the opening of blind eyes are miracles.

We are left, then, with two explanations of this miracle in John's Gospel, the natural and the supernatural. John indeed supported both at the same time. In essence, John said, *No matter how you cut it, God performed a bona fide miracle.* A naturalistic explanation does not eliminate the supernatural elements of the miracle. Nor can a magical explanation eliminate the greater miracle of God's ongoing, ordinary, providential care for His people.

As we continue reading John we will see that this dual emphasis upon the natural and the supernatural is in keeping with his concern for the dual nature of Jesus Christ, Son of Man and Son of God, human and divine. The tension of this dichotomy runs deep in John's Gospel. Jesus was both human and divine. He was of the natural order, and of God's supernatural order—both simultaneously. John's description of this miracle proclaims clearly both of the poles of this dichotomy. John will continue to hold Christ's humanity and His divinity in tension, as must we. To deny either side, either explanation, is to fall into error, to miss something significant about this miracle.

The application is the same for us today. We must proclaim Christ's humanity and His divinity. We must subscribe to both the natural and the supernatural explanations of God's providence. In our own lives we must look for all the natural provisions that God has blessed us with, and at the same time we must cling to the hope of God's miraculous intervention, that God will act outside of our own understanding, that God will heal our blindness. Today that miraculous intervention may come in any form, just as it has in the past. But the highest supernatural hope that Christians cling to is the return of Jesus Christ our Lord.

When He finally returns there will be both natural and supernatural explanations of His return. We can expect that because of the dual nature of Jesus Christ—His humanity and divinity. But in the final analysis the explanations people come up with do not matter. The explanations do not alter the reality. Explanations will come and go. What matters is the reality of God's providence, given through Christ to all His people forever. The reality of the greater miracle is the providence of God's living Word, Jesus Christ. Praise be to God!

Liturgy

One other thing regarding these verses to notice is that the immediate cause of the miracle was Jesus, who "took the loaves, and when He had given thanks He distributed them" (v. 11). It is significant that Jesus employed the communion liturgy to open the stores of God's provision for His people. Jesus will address the communion implications of this miracle in verse 35 of this same chapter. There He teaches that He is "the bread of life." The feeding of the five thousand points to the establishment of Christ's church through Holy Communion. There Jesus explains that God feeds His church with "the bread of life," Jesus Christ, God's Word, by His eternal providence.

Note also to whom Jesus distributed the loaves. He distributed them to the disciples, to the Twelve. And they in turn distributed them to the people. The order of distribution is significant. It prefigures and establishes order in the church. It proclaims that God's provision comes in an orderly fashion. The people did not pounce upon the food like hungry dogs. God created order in the wilderness. And the order was part and parcel of the miracle. The order was a reflection of the authority of His church.

Part of the miracle was the order that Jesus brought to the crowd. God provided through the order. God's order is not incidental, but necessary. Everywhere that God performed miracles He did so in an orderly fashion. God's miracles always create order. God's order is a miraculous gift of both creation and providence. God's order is both natural and supernatural.

The application here is that we disregard God's order at our own peril. Jesus established order in His church as God established order in His world, an order for worship and distribution of gifts, an order for authority and the use of gifts. When churches violate God's order they cannot expect God's provision. Perhaps this is why Christ's church languishes in our day, fragmented and broken across the landscape.

Perhaps revival is waiting for the churches to return to God's established order. Perhaps there is an order without which revival cannot happen.[6] Perhaps the church as an organization is obliged to

---

6   I do not mean to suggest that there is a single correct ecclesiastical order. Scripture provides ample room for a variety of church polities. No one polity fits every circum-

be faithful to God's order, just as the individuals who compose the church are obliged to remain in a living, vital, personal relationship with Jesus Christ. Surely that's the key to sustainable revival—a living, vital, personal relationship with Jesus Christ within the established order of God's church.

---

stance. Nonetheless, within those individual polities there is to be an emphasis upon authority and relationship. There is freedom within certain limits. But our current situation may well be that in all church polities there has been disregard for the authority and relationships that are necessary to promote and sustain ordinary faithfulness.

Walking on Water

One Night On The Sea

"Perceiving then that they were about to come and take him by force to make him king, Jesus withdrew again to the mountain by himself. When evening came, his disciples went down to the sea, got into a boat, and started across the sea to Capernaum. It was now dark, and Jesus had not yet come to them. The sea became rough because a strong wind was blowing. When they had rowed about three or four miles, they saw Jesus walking on the sea and coming near the boat, and they were frightened. But he said to them, 'It is I; do not be afraid.' Then they were glad to take him into the boat, and immediately the boat was at the land to which they were going." —John 6:15-21

When the people had eaten their fill, and saw the twelve baskets of fragments that were left over, they were in the wake of a miracle (*semeion*). A *semeion*, whether or not supernatural phenomena are attached, makes known or points to God's presence. As well as being a miracle, the feeding of the five thousand was an historical sign that pointed to Jesus as Messiah. This could not be made more clear than by the fact that immediately following the miracle the people were willing even "by force to make (Jesus) king" (v. 15).

The intention of the crowd was to proclaim Jesus king, much as the kings and judges of old were chosen to rout Israel's enemies. Given the political sensitivities of the day, those who wanted Jesus to be king were probably ready to move against Rome to reassert the old independence of the Israelite kingdom.

The feeding of the five thousand was not simply a display of Christ's awesome power, nor merely an expression of humanitarian concern, it was a political event with an economic lesson. The people saw it as a political event, and it is impossible that Jesus would not have known that they did. As a result they were ready to proclaim Him king. He had upset the political apple cart of Israel from that secluded spot on the shores of the Sea of Galilee with a demonstration of political power. Jesus had inserted Himself into Jerusalem politics while out in the wilderness.

THE FAILURE

The people had been fed in more ways than one that day. Their hearts and souls had been nourished with a new found hope, and they liked it. They wanted more. But it is unlikely that they were filled with a genuine desire for the Lord. They were not seeking salvation because they had been convicted of sin. Rather, John tells us that their desire to make Jesus king was a desire for political independence. They were tired of the oppression of Rome. They were self-motivated, politically motivated, not God-motivated, not theologically motivated.

The conviction of sin is always the key to the success of the gospel. Where people are convicted of sin, the gospel is well received. Where people are not convicted of sin, the gospel falls flat. Where there is no conviction of sin, people do not believe that they need the gospel. So, they ignore it.

Knowing what He knew about the motivation of the crowd, Jesus withdrew. He was not convinced of the faithfulness of the crowd, or of their conviction of sin. He knew that many would soon fall away (John 6:66). John records no motive for His withdrawal, although Matthew (14:23) and Mark (6:46) said that He went apart to pray. Gospel success is always the result of prayer. As human beings we are unable to convict anyone of sin. That is the prerogative and function of the Holy Spirit. We can only add our prayers for the Holy Spirit to bring conviction to the unrepentant.

We can infer, since the people were about to come and take Jesus "by force," that He did not want to go. He refused their offer of kingship, and retired to the mountains. They offered Him greatness, and He showed them humility. He wanted nothing of human greatness. In everything He revealed His humility and called His people to do likewise.

The Sea

That same evening Jesus was seen walking on the Sea of Galilee. What in the world does that mean? John's treatment of this supernatural phenomenon is fascinating. With the hope of understanding it, we will again look carefully at what Scripture says, and at what it doesn't say. Again, there is no reason to think that this story is not historical.

The story begins that very evening. That would imply that the feeding had not been far from shore. Certainly less than a day's walk, more likely only a few hours at most.

Why did the disciples go to the sea after the feeding? Jesus wanted to pray alone, and sent them away. At this point, the disciples were more in agreement with the crowd who wanted to crown Jesus king than they were in agreement with Jesus' desire for humble service. Jesus didn't want the disciples to follow the interests of the crowd in calling for Him to be king. He wanted them to follow Him, not the crowd. So, He sent them away, away from Him and away from the crowd. Whether they were sent on an errand, or to protect them from being influenced by the crowd, or to teach them a lesson, we don't know. All we know is that they were going to Capernum.

The disciples sailed toward Capernaum without Jesus, who was off praying alone. The synoptic gospels situated the miracle of the feeding of the five thousand near Bethsaida, but John placed it near Tiberias. Some confusion and difference of opinion among the commentators has arisen about this. But because its significance has no practical application, we will let them wrestle with the discrepancy. We will only assume that John sent them to Capernaum because it is the simple reading of John.

Notice that it was evening and "already dark" when Jesus was seen on the water. Imagine the Sea of Galilee in the dark. A clear night and a bright moon would be required to see anything at all. So, we assume the presence of these factors. Winds and storms are usually associated with clouds, which would have obscured the moon and made it more difficult to see anything on the sea.

That region was particularly susceptible to sudden high winds sweeping down the valleys and onto the sea. Such winds do not necessarily require clouds. Scripture doesn't mention clouds, only wind. So, we will assume a clear moonlit night and high winds. High winds also involve a rapid temperature change in that high winds are associated with the movement of weather fronts.

Verse 19 tells us that they had been rowing for three or four miles. According to Matthew and Mark the wind was contrary, against them, so they rowed rather than sailed. The three or four miles they rowed would have placed them sufficiently far from the shore that they could not have mistook Jesus walking on the shore. Nor with that much wind could they have heard Him speak unless He was near them.

John said, "they saw (*theōreō*) Jesus walking on the sea" (v. 19). But did he mean that they saw the Jesus they knew personally walking with His own feet upon the Sea of Galilee? Such a thing flies in the face of common sense. So we will engage in a word by word analysis to help us understand exactly what John said.

John used a different word for *see* than did Matthew and Mark. Matthew and Mark used *eidō* where John used *theōreō*. By using *theōreō* John may have been trying to communicate something special, something different from the other reports of this story. *Theōreō* is translated mostly as *see*, but also as *behold, perceive, consider,* and *look on*. It carries the meaning of contemplating the object seen, of thinking deeply about it. John's word conveys more of a theoretical seeing, not to suggest that such a sight was imaginary, but that the seeing of it required an interpretation of the event, an understanding about it—if you *see* what I mean. Remember, it's John's word, not mine. I'm just telling you what it means.

John said that they *saw* Jesus walking on the sea, but was He actually walking. The Greek word translated *walking* is *peripateō*. It is the same word Jesus used when He commanded the invalid of thirty-eight years at the Pool of Bethesda to rise, take up his bed and walk (*peripateō*, John 5:8). There, as we saw, Jesus commanded the man to walk in faith, to walk the walk of faith, to be otherwise occupied. And here on the sea Jesus was Himself seen walking the walk of faith upon the water. We don't want to make too much of this, but neither can we ignore it.

Jesus was seen walking in faith on the sea. But did John mean *sea*, as in large body of water? The Greek word for *sea* (*thalassa*) always and only means *sea*, as in a great body of water. John meant that they saw Jesus waking in faith on the Sea of Galilee. But how can that be? The image is so contrary to our normal expectations and perceptions. What sense can we make of it? Let's interpret it literally.

The Reality

Imagine the reality of Jesus walking on the sea during a raging wind storm. The wind would have stirred up waves several feet high, reeling and rolling, as waves do. That's the image that John painted. Would Jesus' feet float upon the waves like a boat? It would seem a feat of great skill just to maintain one's balance if such were the case. Would Jesus slide down the waves like a surfer? Water is slippery. Would his feet hold fast to where He planted them, climbing over them like sand dunes? Whatever scenario you choose—surfing or climbing, it is a difficult image to understand. No such details are provided. Nonetheless, at some point Jesus climbed into the fishing boat with the disciples.

What was John trying to tell us? How can we understand such a thing? The best sense that I can make of it is that John was saying that there is more to Jesus than meets the eye. Our eyes alone cannot explain this story. There is more to this story than what appears on the surface. There is something here that is beyond our understanding.

As much as John has encouraged natural explanations to account for Jesus' miracles, here He demonstrates the utter inadequacy of natural explanations. Here John calls his readers to a serious consideration of the reality of the supernatural. In fact, he devotes the remainder of this chapter, and several others, to an explanation of it.

Biblical scholars provide a wealth of information and opinion about this walking on the sea event. Where Moses parted the sea, Jesus walked upon it. Many scholars think that John alludes to the advent of Jesus Christ as a kind of second exodus. Where Moses separated the sea, Jesus did not. If the ancient Israelites had been able to walk on the sea, Moses would not have had to part it.

Whatever was going on as Jesus was seen walking on the sea, it is deep, profound, and mysterious. There are a wealth of implications! But whatever you think actually happened, this story cannot be ignored. Nor can it be explained as anything other than a miracle—a supernatural event, and a sign that pointed to Jesus being the Messiah of God.

However we understand this miracle—or don't, the story continued. Jesus said to His disciples, "It is I; do not be afraid" (v. 20). We need not fear for a lack of understanding, nor because we think it other worldly. Our first response to the unknown is usually fear. People cannot think clearly when they are afraid, so Jesus said, "do not be afraid." While fear is the beginning of wisdom, too much fear short circuits our ability to think clearly.

Once the disciples determined that it really was Jesus, they eagerly received Him into the boat with them. Having done that, they knew they were not dealing with a ghost. They physically hauled Him into the boat. They touched and handled Him. He was flesh and blood. This was no ghost walking on the sea.

Once Jesus had been identified and they had received Him, they continued their journey without further delay and landed at Capernaum—"immediately" (v. 21). As soon as Jesus was in the boat, they arrived at the other shore.

This story of the disciples on the stormy sea is often said to represent the church in this perishing world. Without Jesus disciples are afraid, but with Him they proceed directly to their destination.

The analogy is nice, but it fails to explain the actual event. We have before us a story that makes little sense if we interpret it literally. It contradicts our experience of natural events, yet it is clearly the experience of those who witnessed it. The story is simply a report of what they actually saw, of what they believed they saw. What appears to us to be impossible, the Scriptures clearly affirm. We are called to believe and to trust. But are we called to believe and trust blindly? No. And the reason that we are not called to blind trust is simply that we are in the middle of the story at this point. We have only half a story before us. We are not yet half way through John's gospel story.

We cannot blindly close our eyes to this event. Nor can we abandon either our common sense or our trust in John's veracity.

We must simply reserve judgment of this particular event for the time being. We have no other option. We can't explain it, nor can we dismiss it. Consequently, we are called to reserve judgment and read on. Our usual categories of understanding have been challenged, shattered actually. We are compelled to continue the story in order to solve this mystery. Half a house cannot keep out the cold. Half a meal cannot satisfy our hunger. Half a gospel can only lead us astray. We have embarked upon a spiritual journey, and at this point we must continue. Our trust or faith must exceed our understanding.

The application of this story at this point is simply that half-way measures are always unsatisfactory and inadequate. Christians are not called to meet Jesus half-way. Christians are not called to make up their own explanations of Jesus' miracles. Christians are called to study God's Word and to allow God's Word to establish them in the faith. Christians are called to go the extra mile, to go all the way—and then some. We are called outside of ourselves. We are called to trust beyond what we know, beyond what we think we know. We are called to amazement. This story reveals the poverty of our explanations for the activities of God, who is full of surprises that are beyond our understanding.

The Works of God

"On the next day the crowd that remained on the other side of the sea saw that there had been only one boat there, and that Jesus had not entered the boat with his disciples, but that his disciples had gone away alone. Other boats from Tiberias came near the place where they had eaten the bread after the Lord had given thanks. So when the crowd saw that Jesus was not there, nor his disciples, they themselves got into the boats and went to Capernaum, seeking Jesus. When they found him on the other side of the sea, they said to him, 'Rabbi, when did you come here?' Jesus answered them, 'Truly, truly, I say to you, you are seeking me, not because you saw signs, but because you ate your fill of the loaves. Do not labor for the food that perishes, but for the food that endures to eternal life, which the Son of Man will give to you. For on him God the Father has set his seal.' Then they said to him, 'What must we do, to be doing the works of God?' Jesus answered them, 'This is the work of God, that you believe in him whom he has sent.'" —John 6:22-29

Not only had Jesus been seen walking upon the sea, but the multitude who had just been fed bread and fish added their testimony to the miracle of Jesus walking upon the sea. They, too, wondered how Jesus had crossed the sea.

Jesus had sent the disciples to Capernaum, but He had gone to the mountains to pray. Then, during a wind storm at sea, Jesus was not only seen walking upon the water, but He got into the boat with the disciples and went to Capernaum. The testimony of the crowd was that there had been only one boat where they were and that Jesus had not entered it with the disciples. Their testimony served as a kind of proof that Jesus walked on the sea.

Shortly thereafter other boats had come to Capernaum from Tiberias, looking for Jesus. The other boats seem to have transported those who were following Jesus to Capernaum. Their testimony was that Jesus had not gone with the disciples, nor was He anywhere to be found. So they sailed to Capernaum in search of Him. Their testimony was that they didn't know how Jesus had gotten to Capernaum. He hadn't gone with the disciples, nor with those who came later, and no other boats were available.

That is why they were astonished to find Him at Capernaum, even though they had gone there to find Him. They simply followed the disciples to Capernaum, hoping that they would know where Jesus had gone, or that He would catch up with them there.

> "Other boats from Tiberias came near the place where they had eaten the bread after the Lord had given thanks." (John 6:23).

Notice how verse 23 phrases the memory of the feeding of the five thousand. There is an intentional linking of this event of Jesus crossing the sea with the miraculous feeding and Jesus giving thanks. The miraculous feeding was linked to His giving thanks. That is an important insight, but it seems out of place. It seems to certify that those who were following Jesus knew about the miraculous feeding.

God's providential care was initiated (or extended) by the act of Jesus giving thanks. It was Jesus who gave thanks, and Jesus who produced the miracle of the bread and fish. We cannot expect to reproduce such a miracle. But we can expect that God's providential care and our perception of that care will be greatly increased by our giving thanks. Scripture commands Christians to be thankful (1 Thessalonians 5:18; Colossians 3:17). Thankfulness in all things is the key to the blessings of faithfulness. Those who are thankful are also faithful. Faithfulness without thankfulness is not possible. Those who are faithful are necessarily thankful. And the faithful are prosperous in the blessings of God. The faithful can better see God's provisions and care for His people.

Grace is freely given, but once it is received the appropriate response is thankfulness. People cannot be thankful unless and until they have received God's grace. Therefore, grace does not come in response to human thankfulness, but precedes it as a gift. However, once grace has been received, thankfulness becomes the response (or work) of God's people.

Questions

The first question the crowd asked Jesus, once they found Him, was, "Rabbi, when did You come here?" (v. 25). They had been looking for Him. Why? To proclaim Him King. They had searched high and low for Him, but could not find Him. They knew that He hadn't gone with the disciples. And they themselves had taken the first boats available. So, they were surprised to find Him in Capernaum. Naturally, they wondered how He had gotten there. Their testimony added substance to the miracle of His walking upon the sea. How else could He have gotten to Capernaum ahead of them?

"Then Jesus answered them" according to verse 26. But in fact Jesus did not answer the question they asked. He had an important response, and He preceded His response with "*Amen, amen,*" to alert them to the truth of what He was about to say.

In what follows Jesus reveals the fact that He knows exactly what is in the heart of every person. We can fool others, but we can't fool Jesus. It is not difficult to deceive people, if you choose to do that. It is particularly easy to deceive ministers, faithful Christians, relatives, and friends. Why? Because they want to believe the best about you. A little outward profession of Christ, or church attendance, and they are taken in. They make every effort to think that you are better than you are. People who are nice and kind think that such behavior helps others to be nice and kind in return. They always want to focus on the positive, and encourage self-esteem.

But you can't fool Jesus. He knows the innermost desires and deceits of your heart. If He doesn't expose your folly in this life, He will uncover it at judgment. There is no escape from judgment for anyone. Our only hope is to give our hearts to Jesus now, to make every effort to conform ourselves to His likeness, and plead for mercy.

Without Belief

Most of the crowd who followed Jesus to Capernaum weren't interested in salvation. They were only interested in their own beliefs. They had seen the "signs" (NKJV), the "miracles" (AV), the *semeion* (Greek). They saw what Jesus had done, but they didn't believe. Jesus noted that the fact that they had witnessed bona fide miracles from the hand of God through the person of the Messiah meant nothing to them. They had gained nothing from the miracles.

The miracles that so many people today think would provide the proof they need in order to believe, did nothing for the crowd. They saw the miracles, but failed to believe. In actuality, miracles do the same thing today as they did in Jesus' day. Miracles can confirm the faith of the faithful, but they do nothing for the faithless. The faithless are not brought to faith by witnessing a miracle. The seeking of miracles is itself a confession of a lack of faith, and the manifestation of miracles will not and cannot produce faith. Those who chase after miracles, chase emptiness. They are barking up the wrong tree.

I say this fully believing in the reality of supernatural miracles. Again, miracles will indeed confirm the faith of the faithful, but will only expose the faithlessness of the faithless. Miracles will draw a crowd, but they won't make them faithful. Most people will turn away in disbelief. Miracles will not bring faith to those who don't have it. Miracles are not a converting factor of faith, and therefore, are not useful for evangelism. Perhaps that's why the Lord doesn't need them among the faithful. If seeing a miracle won't change a person's mind, seeing more of them won't help either.

Response

Jesus' response to the crowd contains four important elements: 1) Something was forbidden, 2) something was commanded, 3) something was promised, and 4) something was declared.

First Jesus forbids Christians to "labor for the food which perishes" (v. 26). The Greek word *brōsis* means generic food, that which nourishes body and soul. This verse could be understood, *Do not labor for that which perishes*, or *Don't hold to temporal and changing values*. Rather, Jesus commands His people to hold eternal values. Hold to that which "endures to everlasting life" (v. 27).

There are many applications of this principle. Some of the applications that we tend to overlook involve the concern for style and fashion. Here Jesus forbids His people to value the ever changing parade of fashionable styles regarding clothes, cars, houses, computers, etc. The concern about style and fashion detracts from what should be the greater concern for God and the eternal things of God.

Fashion and style tend to draw people away from God. The more people are concerned about fashion, the less they are concerned about God. Such worldly concerns encourage people to buy new clothes, cars, houses, computers, etc.—not because they need them, but in order to be stylish, to be on the cutting edge. Time and money spent on fashionable pursuits is time and money that doesn't support God's work. The attention and concern given to such matters is attention and concern that are drawn away from the Lord. God's people are here forbidden to labor for that which perishes, to labor for the temporary.

God's people are also commanded to labor for that which endures unto everlasting life. God's people are forbidden the temporal values of style and fashion, and are commanded to stake their tent on the Rock of Ages. Whatever "that which endures unto eternal life" (v. 27) means, it begins in Scripture. Jesus Christ is revealed in Scripture. Consequently, the eternal values that God's people are commanded to take up require the study of the Bible. It all begins there.

Wrongheaded

Thirdly, Scripture promises that the Son of Man (Jesus) will give that which endures to everlasting life. The verb is in the future tense, it is a promise. Jesus Christ *will* supply everything needed. Who was Jesus talking to in this story? He was talking to those who followed Him for the wrong reasons.

He was talking to people with good intentions, good-hearted people who had some wrong ideas about Jesus and about faith generally. Jesus told the crowd that they were wrong. They were filled with wrong ideas and wrong desires. They wanted the wrong things in life. They valued the wrong things. They gave their money and their time to the wrong things. Earlier Jesus had spoken in the same way to the Pharisees (John 5).

Here He admonished His *followers*. It is important to see that Jesus admonished His followers. He offended those who followed Him. These were people who had followed Him across the sea. These were followers, people who had gone out of their way to follow Jesus. But Jesus told them the truth: they were mistaken! These were the people to whom Jesus would say at judgment,

> "Not everyone who says to Me, 'Lord, Lord,' shall enter the kingdom of heaven, (only) he who does the will of My Father in heaven" (Matthew 7:21).

These people thought they were doing right, but Jesus corrected them. Not because He was angry at them, but because He loved them and wanted them to be saved. But to be saved they needed to repent and be converted. They needed to turn their lives around and be conformed to Christ.

Why did they need to follow Christ alone, and not some other? Why is Christ the only Savior? Because God said so. Because Christ obeyed unto death. Because Christ completed His mission of atonement. Because Christ is God incarnate. Because only Christ fulfilled Scripture. Because unity has only one head.

Still confused, still unconverted, still without understanding, they asked, "What shall we do" (v. 28)? They didn't know, and they admitted it. But they were still caught up in works-righteousness. The spirit of works-righteousness is tenacious. Every religion known to man demands that people do something in order to be acceptable to God and heaven.

Hindus work their way up the ladder of reincarnation. Buddhists must escape bondage to reincarnation by merging with the void. Those who follow Confucius must please the departed spirits of their ancestors. American Indians seek to appease the spirits. Works-righteous Christians (and others who follow the Protestant work ethic) are convinced that they must cleanse themselves of impurities, or otherwise do something to become morally acceptable to God.

Only Jesus teaches that it is all a bunch of hogwash, because you can't get there (to God) from here (human effort). Only Jesus says that human beings of themselves cannot do what God's requires. Only Jesus the Messiah of God did for us what we cannot do for ourselves. Jesus has given His righteousness that His people may come before God at judgment, clothed in His authority. By His authority the grace of mercy has been poured out to the undeserving. But only by His authority, and only upon those under His authority.

But still, so many people—Christians and non Christians alike—mistakenly think that they have to do something to receive God's grace, mercy, and salvation. When Peter preached at Pentecost "they were cut to the heart, and said to Peter and the rest of the apostles, 'Men and brethren, what shall we do'" (Acts 2:37)? When Paul and Silas sang at midnight and God loosed their chains, the guard asked, "Sirs, what must I do to be saved" (Acts 16:30)?

Believe

Jesus knew that people would respond this way. He knew how stuck in their ways people get. So, even though He would do it all, He said, (as the apostles said) *believe*.

> "This is the work of God, that you believe in Him whom He sent" (v. 29).

God's work is to make you believe. The question about what to do is not bad or wrong in itself, because it points to salvation. It's a natural question. But we must remember that salvation comes by the supernatural grace of God alone, and not by anything that people do, not even the decision to believe can cause salvation to happen (Mathew 7:21).

Human decisions are fickle. To stake salvation upon human decisions is to invite a decision for salvation one day, and the damnation of indecision or a change of mind the next. Belief is not a decision people can make apart from the power and presence of the Holy Spirit, but is the reality of God's Spirit joined with Christ's Spirit through the power of the Holy Spirit influencing the hearts and minds of God's people.

Salvation is not something to be decided upon, but to be received. To think in terms of decisions, moves the reality of salvation from the heart to the head. It turns it into an abstraction. Salvation does not begin in the head, but in the heart. Salvation is God's idea and God's action. It's His plan, and He sent Jesus to fulfill it. God has already made all the necessary decisions, and provides salvation for those who will receive it.

If you have never told God that you are willing to receive His salvation, won't you do so now? In your own words, in your own mind, in your own way, tell God that you are willing to receive Jesus, and have your life turned around. The issue is not whether or not you will do it, but whether you actually *want* to do it, because if you really *want* to do it, it's already been done. God does not give people new decisions, He gives them new hearts, new desires.

What Sign?

"So they said to him, 'Then what sign do you do, that we may see and believe you? What work do you perform? Our fathers ate the manna in the wilderness; as it is written, "He gave them bread from heaven to eat."'" —John 6:30-31

Most of those who had followed Jesus across the sea to Capernaum had been among the five thousand who had been fed bread and fish the day before. They were aware of two miracles: 1) the feeding and 2) the walking upon the water. And surely among the crowd were those who had witnessed some of the other miracles of Jesus, as well. Surely some had been at the wedding, and some at the pool of Bethesda. Surely the stories about Jesus had reached many ears. Yet, this incredulous question leaped out at Jesus from the crowd.

"What sign (*sēmeion*) will You perform then, that we may see it and believe" (v. 30)?

J.C. Ryle appropriately responded,

"Nothing so thoroughly reveals the hearts of men as a summons to believe on Christ. Exhortations to work excite no prejudice and enmity. It is the exhortation to believe that offends."[1]

The appeal of works-righteousness is that people (mistakenly) think that they can earn God's acceptance themselves, and thereby they don't have to submit to Jesus.

---

1 Ryle, p. 364.

The works-righteous remain in control, but those who believe on Christ must surrender control of their lives. It is the call to submit their lives and their understanding to Christ that offends the self-righteous. In submission it is no longer *my* perception that guides me, but *God's*—no longer *my* will, but God's, no longer my interpretation, but God's that is important to me.

The word *You* is emphatic in the Greek. It has a special emphasis. The question asked, *Who do you think* **you** *are that you can talk to us this way? What evidence of God's Messiahship can you produce?* Sarcasm dripped from the question. They thought it presumptive for Jesus to assume to know God's perspective.

Prove It!

The unconverted always want proof first. *Give me proof and then I'll believe,* they say. But faith does not require proof, genuine faith is proof for those who believe. If proof was a prerequisite, you would end up with science, not faith. The unregenerate demand sight from blind eyes before the healing of their blind eyes. But vision—spiritual seeing—is the consequence of faith. Spiritual insight is the result of faith, not its prerequisite. The demand for proof inverts God's order of things. The proof of faith comes from belief. Believing provides the eyes of faith, and the eyes of faith then see the evidence of faith everywhere.

There is a difference between believing Jesus and believing *on* Jesus. People may think that *believing on* is just a curiosity of archaic language, but there is more to it than that. To believe Jesus is to concede that He speaks the truth. To believe *on* Jesus is saving faith. It is the faith that trusts beyond the limits of one's own understanding. Satan believes Jesus, but fails to believe *on* Him. We may believe John's testimony that Jesus is the Christ, but we do not believe *on* John. To believe *on* Christ is to place your belief onto or into Him. Belief then rests in or on Jesus. Jesus is the Rock upon which faith sits. Saving faith is belief that is utterly dependent upon Jesus.

"What work will You do" (v. 30)? the crowd asked Jesus. Were these not the same people who just followed Jesus across the Sea of Galilee? The same people whose testimony gave added evidence for the miracle of His walking upon the sea? The same people who had eaten the miraculous bread and fish? Didn't they just witness two miracles?

Why do they now seek another? The question was asked as if they had no idea who Jesus was, as if they knew nothing about the miracles He had already worked, as if He had no credentials at all with them. These were the people who had gone out of their way to follow Jesus to Capernaum! What is going on here? Why was such a question even asked?

Herd Mentality

The people had been taken captive by a kind of mob mentality. When people get caught up in a crowd, mob mentality takes over. Mob mentality is a sociologically documented phenomena related to peer pressure. People act differently in a crowd than they do alone or with a small group of friends. The phenomena of mob mentality is very real, and we are all susceptible to it. Mob mentality tends to bring everyone in the crowd down to the lowest common moral denominator. Crowds are fickle and impulsive. Clear thinking is never done in or by crowds.

Crowds are easily manipulated by cunning people. A manipulated crowd demanded the crucifixion of Jesus, and the stoning of Stephen. Mob psychology has always been a tool of the wicked. The modern world has made a fine art of it through the study of mass media.

The old adage, "safety in numbers," is true to a certain extent. But beyond a certain point, the larger the numbers, the less safety there is. Crowds are blinded by herd mentality. They are guided by peer pressure and group-think, and we all know the power and moral poverty of peer pressure, of the foolish leading the foolish. Biblical morality calls people out from the influence of peer pressure. The Bible calls individuals to take a stand for God apart from the crowd.

Perhaps this is why God invented writing. For the most part, the engagement of the written word—reading—is a solitary and personal affair. The reading of Scripture is a matter between the reader and God.

Biblical morality is not a program of mass movements. It is not a product of mass manipulation. Rather, God trains individuals for the accomplishment of His will, and He often takes them out into the wilderness away from other people for a while in the process. Whenever God called large numbers of people in the Bible, they were always bound to the authority and accountability of smaller groupings of people organized and governed by biblical principles.

> "Moses chose able men out of all Israel, and made them heads over the people: rulers of thousands, rulers of hundreds, rulers of fifties, and rulers of tens" (Exodus 18:25).

Saul and David organized their armies with captains of thousands, hundreds, fifties, and tens. In the story of the feeding of the five thousand Mark reported that the people "sat down in ranks, in hundreds and in fifties" (Mark 6:40). God does not gather people outside of or apart from the structures and relationships of biblical authority and accountability. He knows better.

Evangelism

One of the problems of modern mass evangelism and mass rallies is that they undermine the authority and accountability of the local church. That's not their intention, but it is a common outcome. The media is able to reach into local churches, bypassing the structures of local church authority and accountability, of protection and preservation, that have been ordained by God. People can and do watch whatever television programs or listen to whatever radio programs or buy whatever books they want. People are then spiritually effected by these things without regard for the oversight of their own local pastors and elders (assuming that biblical relationships are functional at all within local churches—and too often they are not). Mass media bypasses the shepherding function of local pastors and elders.

Local pastors and elders, the ordained guardians of sound teaching and orthodox doctrine in the church, are bypassed by modern mass media. New teaching and new doctrines are brought into the church without regard for those charged to "keep the traditions" (1 Corinthians 11:2). Peter warned,

> "beware lest you also fall from your own steadfastness, being led away with the error of the wicked" (2 Peter 3:17).

Jude warned that certain men had crept into the church unawares (Jude 1:4). The book of Revelation predicts that the serpent of old, called the Devil and Satan, will deceive the whole world (Revelation 12:9). If we are living in the end times—and we are, this deception is already upon us. The definition of being deceived requires that you don't know you are deceived, because when you learn that you have been deceived, you correct it.

At best, the unrestrained mixing of various theological and denominational teaching results in confusion. Take a little Baptist teaching here, Presbyterianism there, frost it with Pentecostalism, bake it in the oven of liberalism, and you have a mess. At the very least the result of denominational interpenetration regarding theology will produce internal theological contradictions. What we have in the churches today is mass theological confusion. In this way mass evangelism, mass rallies, and mass media tend to confuse theological understanding and undermine the authority and accountability of the local churches.

I realize that most local churches do not function by biblical structures of authority and accountability at the present time. Nor do most people actually live by biblical principles. And so most people don't realize that they are already actively engaged in violations of biblical authority and accountability. That in itself is a serious problem. But the solution of the problem of the lack of biblical organization at the local church level is not mass evangelism, not mass rallies, nor mass media presentations, but the implementation of biblical principles—biblical authority and accountability—in the local churches.

Mass media products and events do not strengthen the local church, but produce the opposite effect. Authority is transferred from the local church to the organizational structures and leaders of the mass movement, to some other pastor, preacher, or theologian. The organizers of the mass movement gain authority and the credibility that results in the sales of their various products at the expense of the authority of the local churches. In addition, beliefs are imposed upon local church members by forces outside and beyond the control of the local churches, thus undermining the authority and accountability that should belong to local churches.

The result of this process is that church members often have greater allegiance to Billy Graham or whoever, than they do to their own pastor. When that happens the God-ordained relationship between pastor and congregation is undermined, and the whole church suffers.

The problem is that you and I are not in a personal relationship with Billy Graham or whoever—and we can't be. The receiving end of the relationship with mass media personalities is one-sided, and biblical accountability requires a mutual relationship. Real relationships involve give and take, but you can't have a relationship with your TV. You can't be accountable to a book. A person is required. Even when parachurch organizations offer a person to fill the accountability role, it is usually a person outside the structure of the local church, which creates the same problem. Nor will the interactivity of the Internet solve this problem. People need to be accountable face to face. Social media is just another kind of mass media.

If its not the message of the media superstars that causes the problem, it is the methods that they use—mass evangelism and rallies, called and organized outside of and apart from local church structures. Each of the media superstars has a particular doctrinal emphasis. And when their emphasis is different from that of a local church it creates an unnecessary conflict.

> "There is a way that seems right to a man, But its end is the way of death" (Proverbs 14:12).

The problem is that most church members will sooner listen to Billy Graham or whoever, before they will listen to their own pastor. When a theological difference arises, people follow their favorite Christian media star over their church or pastor or elders. They assume that a larger market share insures the truth of mass media, as if market share and truth share are the same thing. But by doing so, local church authority and accountability are diminished. People, like sheep, tend to follow the crowd.

The point is that God has ordained structures of authority and accountability, biblically ordained relationships, to work through the local church, and to ignore or avoid those structures is to operate outside of God's will for the local church.

In the story before us the crowd was not guided by the structures of God's Word, but by mob mentality. As such, they were unable to see the Messiah before their eyes. They were unable to see that Jesus had already given them all the miracles they needed to prove His Messiahship.

Like the Israelites in the dessert, they quickly turned their backs on the Lord and longed for "the cucumbers, and the melons, and the leeks, and the onions, and the garlic" of Egypt (Numbers 11:5). Rather than seeking the "food which endures to everlasting life"— spiritual food, they sought "food which perishes" (v. 27). They were more concerned for their stomachs than for their souls. Of this situation, J.C. Ryle wrote (in 1869!),

> "Surely when we see such proofs of the extreme dullness and deadness of man's heart, we have no reason to be surprised at what we see among professing Christians."[2]

The church has radically changed since this was written, and has fallen into increasing disarray because of it. Examine the following Statement of Doctrine, written by Charles Hodge (1797-1878) in order to see how much the church has changed over the last century. For many years Hodge's *Systematic Theology* was a standard text in Protestant seminaries.

Statement of Doctrine[3]

The Augustinian scheme includes the following points:

1. That the glory of God, or the manifestation of his perfections, is the highest and ultimate end of all things.
2. For that end God proposed the creation of the universe, and the whole plan of providence and redemption.
3. That He placed man in a state of probation, making Adam, his first parent, his head and representative.
4. That the fall of Adam brought all his posterity into a state of condemnation, sin, and misery, from which they are utterly unable to deliver themselves.

---

2 Ryle, p. 364.
3 *Systematic Theology*, Three Volumes, by Charles Hodge, Eerdmans Publishing Co., Grand Rapids, Michigan, reprint 1995, p. 333.

5. From the mass of fallen men God elected a number innumerable to eternal life, and left the rest of mankind to the just recompense of their sins.
6. That the ground of this election is not the foresight of anything in the one class to distinguish them favorably from the members of the other class, but the good pleasure of God.
7. That for the salvation of those thus chosen to eternal life, God gave his own Son, to become man, and to obey and suffer for his people, thus making a full satisfaction for sin and bringing in everlasting righteousness, rendering the ultimate salvation of the elect absolutely certain.
8. That while the Holy Spirit, in his common operations, is present with every man, so long as he lives, restraining evil and exciting good, his (God's) certainly efficacious and saving power is exercised only in behalf of the elect.
9. That all those whom God has thus chosen to life, and for whom Christ specially gave Himself in the covenant of redemption, shall certainly (unless they die in infancy), be brought to the knowledge of the truth, to the exercise of faith, and to perseverance in holy living unto that end.

Such is the great scheme of doctrine known in history as the Pauline, Augustinian, or Calvinistic, taught, as we believe, in the Scriptures, developed by Augustine, formally sanctioned by the Latin Church, adhered to by the witnesses of the truth during the Middle Ages, repudiated by the Church of Rome in the Council of Trent, revived in that Church by the Jansenists, adopted by all the Reformers, incorporated in the creeds of the Protestant Churches of Switzerland, and of the Palatinate, of France, Holland, England, and Scotland, and unfolded in the Standards framed by the Westminster Assembly, the common representative of the Presbyterians in Europe and America.

It is a historical fact that this scheme of doctrine has been the moving power in the Church; that largely to it are to be referred the intellectual vigor and spiritual life of the heroes and confessors who have been raised up in the course of ages; and that it has been the fruitful source of good works, of civil and religious liberty, and of human progress. Its truth may be evidenced from many different sources.

In the 1600s and early 1700s ninety-five percent of American churches were Reformed, but in our current era these percentages are completely reversed.[4] So, if we understand the traditional theo-

---

4 *The Churching of America, 1776-2005: Winners and Losers in Our Religious Economy*, Roger Finke & Rodney Stark, Rutgers University Press, 2005.

logical debate between Calvinism and Arminianism in its historical form, we must conclude that either the American Protestant church writ large was either wrong at it's inception, or it is wrong now because of this change.

In contrast, I have been arguing for a different conclusion throughout my ministry. That conclusion is that the Bible includes both perspectives and, consequently, we must hold these perspectives in tension. We must understand them in a way that honors the veracity of the Bible. In order to do this the coming chapters will provide an opportunity to compare the contemporary response of many to Jesus today with that of the ancient Jews. The similarities are disturbing.

Bread From Heaven

"Jesus then said to them, 'Truly, truly, I say to you, it was not Moses who gave you the bread from heaven, but my Father gives you the true bread from heaven. For the bread of God is he who comes down from heaven and gives life to the world.' They said to him, 'Sir, give us this bread always.' Jesus said to them, 'I am the bread of life; whoever comes to me shall not hunger, and whoever believes in me shall never thirst. But I said to you that you have seen me and yet do not believe.'" —John 6:32-36

Note that Jesus once again begins with a double *amen* and moves directly to correct a misunderstanding about God's provision of manna (Exodus 16:15). The misunderstanding was the idea that Moses had provided the manna. Jesus corrected them by teaching that it was not Moses who had provided the manna, but God,

"My Father gives you the true bread from heaven" (v. 32).

Not only did Jesus clarify the source of the bread from heaven—that it was God's provision, He clarified the true nature of the bread from heaven. God doesn't simply feed the belly, but God always feeds the soul.

"For the bread of God is He who comes down from heaven and gives life to the world" (v. 33).

What had sustained the Israelites in the desert was not food for their bellies, what really sustained them was God's Word, come down from heaven and given to Moses. It was God's Word that fed them. God's Word has always been the true provision of God, saving and preserving His people unto salvation.

Just as the spirit of sarcasm had infected the crowd as they forgot the miracles Jesus had wrought in their presence, just as they had challenged Him to perform yet another miracle so that they could believe Him, they now sarcastically demanded that Jesus give them such bread. It was as if they had said, *Since you didn't produce a miracle like we asked, then why don't you go ahead and miraculously produce bread. And don't just give it to us today, but supply it forever.* The implication being: *if you think you're so great!*

When Jesus corrected their understanding of Moses' manna, they took offense. Their understanding of the manna miracle had been centered on their bellies and their traditions. They saw no eternal implications of the manna miracle, and took it at face value. But Jesus opened it up to reveal its deeper connotations, to show that it was a foreshadowing of the Messiah, who would provide sustenance and salvation for eternity.

Not only did Moses foreshadow the Messiah, but the very day of the Messiah was upon them, Jesus said. Not only was the desert manna a provision of God's Word, but Jesus said, "I am the bread of life" (v. 35). The new dispensation had come in the Person of Jesus Christ, who stood before them. To move forward with God required the recognition of this historic fact.

The divine provision of the ancient Israelites who wandered in the desert, was given to them as Jesus told them. And in God's new dispensation Jesus Himself was God's bread from heaven. He was God's Word manifest in the flesh. He was God's provision. God was fully manifest in Him, and He would provide sustenance and salvation for God's people.

"He who comes to Me shall never hunger, and he who believes in Me shall never thirst" (v. 35).

Most of the Jews thought that having the Ten Commandments —the Mosaic Law—was the whole of what God would give to His people. The Priests and Scribes helped them interpret the Law and taught them how to live a good life. Striving for the good life motivated them because it provided the goal of faithful living.

The Problem

Here we see that the problem was not simply that the Priests and Scribes dominated and subjected the people to Pharisaical minutia, micromanaging the private lives of the populace. It wasn't simply that the religious leaders tyrannically imposed their religious superstitions upon people. The greater problem was that the people themselves *wanted* what the Pharisees fed them. The people themselves encouraged the Pharisaical leadership of the church. The people had not been oppressed by some sort of pre-Christian innocence, but had themselves encouraged the Pharisaic mindset and their own domination by spiritual tyrants.

Had the Pharisees and Scribes owned a publishing company, and written a host of books proclaiming the merits of the good life based upon Phariseeism and religious superstition, the people would have eaten it up. Such a company would have been a great publishing success. The problem was not just with the religious leaders, but it ran throughout the entire Jewish culture, top to bottom. Wherever people submit to tyrannical domination, they must own their own culpability in the process, particularly since the advent of Christ because Christ has provided the means to overcome tyranny.

It takes two to tango (a kind of dance). Purveyors of false religion cannot hawk their wares unless they are tolerated and supported by people who covet what they teach and buy what they sell. If no one believed it or bought it, such religious nonsense would amount to little more than nothing. The problem in ancient Israel was that they were people with "itching ears" (2 Timothy 4:3). And so are we, little has changed in this regard.

The problem that is evidenced here is that the teaching of the Pharisees had been a raging success among the people of God. The people ate it up, or at least enough of the "right" people ate it up. Phariseeism held sway among those who were politically powerful. They all wanted to live the good life, to get God's blessings.

And then Jesus came along and told them that their highest spiritual aspirations were false, and that He had been sent by God to correct their misunderstandings. Needless to say, He was not well received because he challenged the common beliefs of most people in His day. In essence, He said, *You've got it all wrong. You have misunderstood your own Scriptures. But if you will come to Me and believe on Me, I will set you straight.*

People don't like that message today any more than the ancient Jews did. But we will tolerate it from the lips of Jesus as long as we think that He was talking to someone else, and we are given the freedom to interpret it any way we want. As long as the message can be diverted and/or watered down to mean less than what Jesus intended, we can live with it. But woe to the person who thinks it applies to *us*, and believes and proclaims it literally, as if Jesus was talking to *us!* Woe to the person who presumes to know what Jesus actually meant! Biblically literate orthodox believers are an offense to the self-righteous. People don't like to be wrong, and like it less when they are proven wrong. Thomas, the doubter, said to Jesus,

> "Lord, we do not know where You are going, and how can we know the way?" (John 14:5).

At some point, Thomas heard what Jesus had said to the crowd that day. It finally sunk in. Thomas realized that he had no idea what Jesus was talking about. This confession of Thomas models the beginning of real faith. Before we believe, we are all doubting Thomases.

It is an easier confession for those who come to the Lord directly from unbelief, who don't know the Lord, who are unfamiliar with the Bible and the church. But for those who think they already know—in the church or out, it is a much more difficult confession. It is harder to admit to spiritual blindness than to a simple lack of effort. Thomas had suffered from the former because he had sat under the teaching of the Master, and still didn't get it. Thomas had heard the teaching and doctrines from Jesus' own lips, and didn't get it! Thomas was not Judas, but he had been actively engaged with the disciples in ministry, and didn't get it!

Jesus had fed and addressed many who had taken a detour on their way to Passover. These were "good Jews," like church goers who honor religious holidays like Christmas and Easter. These were people who had studied their Bibles (Old Testament) to some extent, who had provided for the upkeep of the Temple, who paid the

Seeing Beyond Our Expectations

salaries of the Priests and Scribes (tithed). These were not the unchurched, but were at least somewhat faithful, who had been on their way to Passover. And *they* didn't get it!

Blindness

Earlier Jesus had admonished the Priests and Scribes (John 5:19-47), and their pulpits. Here he admonished their flocks, the pews. In this address we will see many of the same themes of faithlessness recurring. Why? Because the religious leaders and their churches were in mutual relationship. They fed upon one another in a way that created a mutual dependency.

Thomas suddenly realized that he had no idea what Jesus was talking about. That is the first step of faith. Knowing Christ requires the prior confession that we don't know Him, that we cannot know Him on our own, that we need help. Our whole society has been steeped in individualism, in self-dependence, and self-reliance. We don't mind giving help where it's needed, but we hate having to receive it.

The first and hardest step toward seeing the light of Christ is the admission of our own blindness. The problem is that people think that they already know and understand Jesus, in spite of the fact that hardly anyone reads the Bible, and fewer yet study it. People tend to think that because they were "raised" in a supposedly Christian society or church that whatever inoculation they received as children is all they need, that what they learned in Sunday School is true or true enough.

Too many people fail to realize that their Sunday School understanding has put Jesus in a box. People have boxed Him out of His real role in their lives. When people think that every interpretation of the Scriptures is equally valid and equally applicable, they do not value God's interpretation, which is the only true interpretation. All opinions are not equal. Some people actually do know more and/or know it better than others. But ultimately, it is God's opinion that counts. And we can know God's opinion. He has written a book!

Ignorance

Thomas suddenly saw his own ignorance. Thomas had been a follower. And more than a casual follower, he had been a disciple, one of the Twelve. Yet he didn't understand. The remarkable thing about Thomas was not his lack of understanding, nor his doubt, but his willingness to confess his own ignorance, his willingness to hang in there with the Lord and to demand that he touch the wounds. Even when he saw the resurrected Lord in person, he knew that he still didn't get it. He knew that he needed the Master's touch. If only all of God's people would be so honest, so willing to be wrong, so willing to learn, so willing to put themselves in the Way of the Lord!

It was the realization of his own ignorance that brought him to the threshold of faith.

> "Lord, we do not know where You are going, and how can we know the way" (John 14:5)?

Jesus answered,

> "I am the way, the truth, and the life. No one comes to the Father except through Me" (John 14:6).

To the Capernaum crowd Jesus said,

> "I am the bread of life. He who comes to Me shall never hunger" (v. 35).

This invitation of Jesus was given to the whole crowd, not part of it. Jesus calls *all* people everywhere to believe *on* Him and have everlasting life! What if everyone actually believed? What a different world it would be. It is possible, and someday it will be true.

> "For God so loved the world that He gave His only begotten Son, that whosoever believes in Him should not perish but have everlasting life" (John 3:16).

Whosoever believes in Him!

> "Come to Me, all you who labor and are heavy laden, and I will give you rest" (Matthew 11:28).

It is not an invitation, it's a command. Come!

Paul wrote to the Romans,

> "For I do not desire, brethren, that you should be ignorant of this mystery, lest you should be wise in your own opinion, that blindness in part has happened to Israel until the fullness of the Gentiles has come in" (Romans 11:25).

If only people would see the glory of Christ! But why can't they see it? Paul tells us that

> "the god of this age has blinded (those) who do not believe, lest the light of the gospel of the glory of Christ, who is the image of God, should shine on them" (2 Corinthians 4:4).

The god of this age has done it. People don't see because they are distracted by false gods and the idolatries thereof. People are too busy with the things of this world, too busy trying to live the good life, too busy earning a living, too busy planning for their retirement, too busy with their hobbies, too busy with the kids, too busy with the gods of this age.

Those who have seen the light of the glory of Christ should not despair for those who have not seen. The temptation to despair is great, but despair comes from misunderstanding. Satan is having a heyday today, and threatens to cast the whole world into death and destruction. It is so easy to be afraid and let fear dominate our thinking. But we are not to fear Satan or his worldliness. We are to fear only the Lord.

> "Behold, the fear of the Lord, that is wisdom, And to depart from evil is understanding" (Job 28:28).

Jesus knew what would happen to His people. Having given the command to the crowd at Capernaum to come to Him, He was well aware of their response.

> "I said to you that you have seen Me and yet do not believe" (v. 36).

The crowd had seen the miracles. They had sat under the teaching of God's Messiah. They had been nourished by the miraculous bread and fish. Yet in spite of all this, they did not believe. And not believing, they did not come.

Jesus invited all, but all did not come. And all will not come. If you are waiting for everyone else to come to Christ first, you will wait forever—in hell! The only real question is, will *you* come? Will *you* believe on Jesus? Will *you* stake your faith on the Rock of Ages? Will *you*, not them, not someone else, but *you*?

God's Will

"But I said to you that you have seen me and yet do not believe. All that the Father gives me will come to me, and whoever comes to me I will never cast out. For I have come down from heaven, not to do my own will but the will of him who sent me. And this is the will of him who sent me, that I should lose nothing of all that he has given me, but raise it up on the last day. For this is the will of my Father, that everyone who looks on the Son and believes in him should have eternal life, and I will raise him up on the last day." —John 6:36-40

Many people lament that they do not know God's will for their lives. The implication being that if only they knew, they would be content or that they would do it. But those who don't know God's will are more often unwilling to make the effort to find it out than they are frustrated by their lack of such knowledge. Knowing God's will is not a difficult thing to do. God has written a Book. What is difficult is living in obedience to God's will. The real problem is not knowing, but submitting to God's will.

The argument can be made that knowledge of God's will requires obedience to what we do know—and it is true! God's will cannot be known unless we are willing to abide by it. And only by abiding by it can it be really known and understood. But as true as that is, it is a chicken-and-the-egg syndrome. Which comes first, knowledge or obedience? You can't have either one without the other, so it would appear that getting started is impossible. It is precisely this problem of beginning a life of faith that Jesus addresses in these verses. Jesus acknowledges that it begins, not with man, but with God.

God Initiates

"All that the Father gives Me will come to me," said Jesus (v. 37).

It is very important that we understand what Jesus has said here. God has given certain people to Jesus, to believe on Him, and all of those will come. That means that effective faith, faith that comes from the power to believe, is a matter of God's giving. But don't despair. If you actually want it, it's already yours. God doesn't withhold it from those who truly want it.

Paul taught that God "chose us in Him before the foundation of the world" (Ephesians 1:4). The natural response to the doctrine of predestination, the response that comes without the guidance of the Holy Spirit, is to withdraw in disgust from the idea that people have no free will in the matter of faithfulness. If God has already chosen "before the foundation of the world" who will be faithful and who will not be, then there seems to be no place for human freedom. People naturally reject this idea because everything in human experience suggests that people do indeed have free will.

But notice that this natural reaction, the reaction of the natural man unaided by the Holy Spirit, is to reject the clear teaching of the Bible. God's Word rightfully claims to be the supreme guide in all matters of faith and living (see 2 Timothy 3:16 & John 10:35). But people naturally make their own experience, their own thoughts, values, and judgments, the supreme guide of their lives, in place of Scripture, just as Eve did in the Garden. That is the problem of idolatry. And God is very concerned about idolatry.

Purpose

Human beings require a central focus for their lives. Without a central purpose life is meaningless, and moral decay sets in. There must always be a center around which faith and life and understanding are organized. Without such a center, organization and understanding are not possible. When God is not given His rightful place at the center of life and understanding, then something else must take that central place. Just as nature cannot tolerate a vacuum, human beings cannot tolerate life without a central focus. Something must fill that central purpose in life.

When God is deposed from His position as the center of life and understanding, something else must fill that central position, or life and understanding will collapse in madness. A central focus is required for human sanity. By contrast the loss of a central focus can produce insanity. Whatever fills that central place is what we worship. Worship is not just coming to a church service, but worship is ordering our lives and our understanding around a central theme or purpose. When that central theme or purpose is God, people engage true worship of God. True worship is more than sitting in church on Sunday. Again, true worship is ordering one's entire life around Jesus Christ. Anything less than that is not true worship.

When people order their lives around money, family, sports, hobbies, etc., then people can rightfully be said to worship those things. Earlier in American history, life indeed revolved around the local church. The local church was the center of the community in early American life. Actually, God was the center, and the church provided a social focal point for a God-centered life.

When the clear teaching of God's Word is rejected for any reason, a vacuum results at the center of life and understanding. We have been created to be worshipful beings. We cannot *not* worship. When God is not at the center of human life, something else will be. When people reject and refuse to worship God they fill the vacuum at the center of their lives with something else—whatever has guided them to reject God. The function of a person's central value system is guidance, the setting of direction and purpose in one's life. Consequently, in the absence of God people allow something else to guide them. Their lives revolve around something. It's always either God or something else.

The normal candidate to take God's place is human understanding, either one's own or that of someone else, someone whom people value and trust. When God is rejected, God's guidance and God's values are also rejected. Other values fill the vacuum left by God. Normally the values of self-esteem and self-concern replace God's values.

People are taught to trust their own personal experience more than God's Word. God's Word is belittled in the contemporary educational establishment and at best ignored by American society. Rugged individualism (personal experience) has always been highly valued in American culture. But Scripture describes the elevation of personal experience as the guiding paradigm in life as foolishness (see Psalm 14:1, Proverbs 12:15, Jeremiah 4:22, Ezekiel 13:3, Romans 1:21, 1 Corinthians 3:1, Galatians 3:3).[5]

Imagine yourself in your car, stopped at a red light. Lightning strikes and the power goes out. The traffic light ceases to function. You are used to obeying the traffic light, but now that it no longer works, what will you obey? Hopefully you will remember the law, if not you will rely upon your own judgment. But when people ignore the law and rely upon their own judgment, accidents happen. Now imagine a policeman (representing human understanding and experience) coming to direct the traffic. The policeman stands above the law and can direct traffic as best he sees fit. He can direct you to ignore a stop sign or a no left turn sign. He is now the law.

The point is that there must be some central authority in life if there is to be order. In terms of life and faith and understanding, that central authority should be God, God's Word. If it is not God, it will be man—ourselves or someone else, some sort of human understanding based upon experience.

My Way

All this is to say that people are well advised not to reject the biblical doctrine of predestination before they have understood it from the biblical point of view. It is most natural to reject God's wisdom from a human standpoint. "For My thoughts are not your thoughts, Nor are your ways My ways," says the Lord in Isaiah 55:8. God doesn't do things like we think He should. God does not think like we do. What we think is right seldom is.

> "There is a way that seems right to a man, But its end is the way of death" (Proverbs 14:12).

Natural human thinking and behavior run directly counter to God. We need to train ourselves not to trust ourselves, but to trust God. The whole point of God's Word is that people are not able to

---

[5] The failure to actually look up these verses indicates the lack of true desire to understand God.

come to a right understanding on their own. God has revealed His will because human beings cannot figure it out on their own. Without God's help the human race is doomed to hell.

To reject the clear teaching of Scripture because you don't understand it, is absolutely contrary to God's teaching. When Scripture is rejected or put aside or ignored because you don't understand it, you have made your own understanding more important than God. When we think that anything is more important than God we are practicing idolatry.

You may not understand *me*, but you cannot afford not to understand *God*. You fail to understand me and there will be no consequence. But to misunderstand God may cost you your life. Whatever a preacher says must always be measured against God's Word, the Bible. And where the preacher strays from God's Word, it is the solemn obligation of God's people to correct him. And where God's people stray from God's Word it is the solemn obligation of the preacher to correct them. Pastor and people are in a mutual accountability relationship, and both must make constant reference to God's Word to insure the fidelity of the church.

Sufficiently

It is also true that what people don't understand they ultimately reject. So, human understanding plays a key role in remaining faithful. The trick is not to reject God before you understand Him rightly. I know that no one can understand God completely, but everyone can understand Him sufficiently. How? It all begins with obedience to God's Word. Understanding is the result of obedience. And obedience is the result of belief. It begins with belief or trust. The more we are obedient to what we do know, the more God will give us to understand. But if we don't use what God has given us, why should He give any more?

Obedience is not possible, of course, without the power and presence of the Holy Spirit. We cannot do it in and of ourselves! God bestows the Holy Spirit and effectually calls those whom He has given to Jesus Christ. Obedience without the Holy Spirit is impossible. Because God has poured out His grace upon undeserving sinners, the obedience of faith and the understanding and assurance of salvation are available to anyone who wants it.

Me, too!

But don't think that just because salvation is all God's doing that there is no corresponding role for human beings to play. Jesus speaks in the very next phrase of the "one who *comes* to" (v. 37) Him. That means that those whom God has given to Jesus must still come to Him. People must come of their own free will. People must freely choose to love and obey God, even though God has predestined them to do so. God has predestined people to follow Jesus of their own free will. This is the clear teaching of Scripture. How can this be true? Because God knows more than we do, and is more powerful than we can imagine. God's perspective is not our perspective, and visa versa.

That doesn't mean that people don't have free will. We do! God has given it to us. Nor does it mean that God has not predestined people to Christ. He has! These two statements appear to be in opposition because they come from two different perspectives. Predestination is God's perspective, and free will is man's perspective. Scripture says that they are not opposed to one another, but that they compliment one another. They are both true and cannot be separated. The faithful must hold these seemingly opposing perspectives together regardless of the tension that may result because it is the practice of holding them together than trains and shapes God's people into faithful servants.

Preservation/Perseverance

Furthermore, Jesus said that those who do come to Him "will by no means (be) cast out" (v. 37). This is the doctrine of the preservation of the saints. But it doesn't mean *once saved always saved*, as if people can do whatever they want once they have made a decision for Christ. Rather, it means that those who persevere in faithfulness, those who continue in Christ, will not forfeit their salvation. This is not a license to do whatever you want in the hope of eventual salvation, but is a simple assurance given to the faithful that continuation in faith will indeed end in eternal salvation. It is an assurance of *faithfulness*, and has no application to the *faithless*.

Jesus has set a model for us to follow in this regard. He was faithful to the end, just as we must be. Jesus was faithful unto death, just as we must be. Whether we die of natural causes, an accident of some sort, or from persecution, we are to follow Jesus by living faithfully day by day. We are to live the faith in obedience, where faithfulness is defined as obedience to Scripture (Romans 1:5; 16:26).

Jesus did not come to do His own will as a human being, but He "came down from heaven…to do the will of (God)" (v. 38). Similarly, we are not to do our own will, but we too are to do the will of God (Matthew 7:21). We are not to live our lives based upon what *we* think is important, but we are to live by what *God* thinks is important. To do less is to live in sin. To do less is to trade salvation for a mess of pottage.

You might think that God asks too much, that you cannot accomplish what He requires of you. And it is precisely because we cannot accomplish what God requires of us that God has sent His Holy Spirit to be our Helper. God does not ask too much. He simply commands obedience, and He has sent the means by which the faithful may obey—the power and presence of the Holy Spirit.

> "You shall receive power when the Holy Spirit has come upon you; and you shall be witnesses to Me in Jerusalem, and in all Judea and Samaria, and to the end of the earth" (Acts 1:8).

If you have received the Holy Spirit, you must pray and study and act upon what has been given to you. If you have not received the Holy Spirit, you are to wait, and pray and study until the Holy Spirit manifests Himself to you. Thus, all action of the church and of God's people originates in God's Holy Spirit. Any action apart from God's Holy Spirit is not God's will. God's will is always obedience to God's Word.

BORN BLIND

Spit & Dirt

"As he passed by, he saw a man blind from birth. And his disciples asked him, 'Rabbi, who sinned, this man or his parents, that he was born blind?' Jesus answered, 'It was not that this man sinned, or his parents, but that the works of God might be displayed in him. We must work the works of him who sent me while it is day; night is coming, when no one can work. As long as I am in the world, I am the light of the world.' Having said these things, he spit on the ground and made mud with the saliva. Then he anointed the man's eyes with the mud and said to him, 'Go, wash in the pool of Siloam' (which means Sent). So he went and washed and came back seeing." —John 9:1-41

This story appears to be incidental in that it occurs as Jesus passed by. He was on His way to somewhere else when He spied a blind man. The Greek word for blind (τυφλός) is the usual word used, and it literally means *opaque* and can be understood literally (physically) or analogically. This is an important issue because we are so tempted to understand it literally, physically, and to ignore the metaphorical allusions and lessons. I'm not suggesting that this person or any other blind person in the biblical stories was not physically blind. But I am suggesting that there are important metaphorical lessons to be learned.

This man had been blind from birth, which means that his blindness was not caused by illness or accident. Whatever people are born with is usually understood to be God-given. So Jesus' disciples asked about the cause of his blindness. Did it result from his sin? Or from the sin of his parents? The question suggests that the common understanding of the time was that birth defects were caused by sin. Consider the teaching of the Ten Commandments:

> "You shall not bow down to them or serve them, for I the LORD your God am a jealous God, visiting the iniquity of the fathers on the children to the third and the fourth generation of those who hate me (Exodus 20:5).

Here it sounds like sin is inherited. But Jesus' answer tells us that the purpose of the man's blindness, and of his healing, has nothing to do with the past. It was not the result of his sin or that of his parents. But rather, the purpose of his blindness was the telling of the story of his healing. The telling of that story then became a witness to the glory of God through the power of Christ. And that incidental encounter would become an important testimony to the power and reality of the gospel. The purpose of his blindness was

> "that the works of God might be displayed in him" (John 9:3).

Clearly, this means that God was the cause of his blindness, which begs the question about whether God causes blindness. Actually, He does:

> "I will bring distress on mankind, so that they shall walk like the blind, because they have sinned against the LORD; their blood shall be poured out like dust, and their flesh like dung" (Zephaniah 1:17).

> "For the word of the cross is folly to those who are perishing, but to us who are being saved it is the power of God. For it is written, 'I will destroy the wisdom of the wise, and the discernment of the discerning I will thwart'" (1 Corinthians 1:18-19).

> "The natural person does not accept the things of the Spirit of God, for they are folly to him, and he is not able to understand them because they are spiritually discerned" (1 Corinthians 2:14).

But so does Satan:

> "In their case the god of this world has blinded the minds of the unbelievers, to keep them from seeing the light of the gospel of the glory of Christ, who is the image of God" (2 Corinthians 4:4).

Jesus then alluded to the lesson that was being taught through this blind man.

> "We must work the works of him who sent me while it is day; night is coming, when no one can work. As long as I am in the world, I am the light of the world" (John 9:4-5).

This man's blindness and healing provided an example of *working* the *work*s of God through Christ. The two Greek words point to the difference between work as an occupation (ἐργάζομαι) and work as a specific task (ἔργον). Jesus' healing of this particular man is an example of the kind of work that the disciples are to be engaged in.

The problem of blindness is that blind people cannot see light. They cannot see or perceive what light reveals. Jesus then provides the lesson that will be taught in this story of the the healing of this blind man.

> "As long as I am in the world, I am the light of the world" (John 9:5)

The lesson is about Jesus, about His presence in the world, and about the light or revelation that He is providing.

The very first thing that Jesus did was totally and completely unexpected. And more than merely unexpected it was, by all measures of civility, disgusting. It would have been as disgusting to them when He did it as it is to us when we think about it.

> "Having said these things, he spit on the ground and made mud with the saliva. Then he anointed the man's eyes with the mud" (John 9:6).

There isn't anything to learn from a literal understanding of spit. So, let's look at it metaphorically. It is such a strange literal idea that Jesus seems to be begging us to see it metaphorically. Spit or saliva is a product of the mouth. Metaphorically, the mouth is the center of many fundamental elements of human activity. It represents consumption, speech, breath, romance, communication, and interaction or conversation. The tongue is in the mouth, and much can also be said about the tongue (James 3:1-12). The mouth and the tongue can serve metaphorically as a door to the soul. The mouth of a river conveys the meaning of a door or gate, from which water—the nectar of life—pours forth.

Jesus then mixed His spit with dirt and made clay. This is reminiscent of the creation of Adam, who was made by God from red clay. Clay or dirt represents the earth and the elements of the earth. So Jesus mixed the product of His mouth with the elements of the earth and applied it to the eyes of the blind man. And He then waxed metaphorical. Yes, of course this actually happened, but the point of it is not the healing of the blind man. It has a much larger point.

And to make that point, Jesus sent the man away. With mud made from Jesus' spit on his eyes Jesus

> "said to him, 'Go, wash in the pool of Siloam' (which means Sent). So he went and washed and came back seeing" (John 9:7).

The point of sending the man to wash publicly was to put the man forward as a public witness for Christ. The pool of Siloam, first built during the reign of Hezekiah (715~686 B.C.), to provide a water supply inside the city of Jerusalem to protect it from a siege, had been reconstructed no earlier than the reign of Alexander Jannaeus (103-76 B.C.). It would have been a major gathering place for ancient Jews making religious pilgrimages to the city, and therefore quite public.

The man did as he had been told, "and came back seeing" (John 9:7). Because this man had been born blind he was known in the community as being blind because he had been seen often begging at various high traffic sites. As a result, a controversy arose about the man's identity. Was this man who could now see really the same man as the blind beggar? Some said *yes*, some said *no*. But the man himself "kept saying, 'I am the man'" John 9:9), as a testimony to his healing.

Naturally, the authorities inquired about how his healing had happened. So, he reported the story in the same way that it has been written by John. Jesus made spit mud, put it on his eyes, and told him to go wash it off—which he did. And now he could see. Those who had been listening then wanted to know where Jesus was, possibly to confirm the story, and possibly to get their share of whatever healing Jesus could provide for them, but more likely they wanted to confront him. But the healed beggar didn't know where Jesus was.

So they brought the healed beggar to the Pharisees—to court, to question him again, and mostly got the same answers, but in addition they learned that the healing had taken place on the Sabbath.

Clearly, the healer had been a professional, and as a professional He did not keep the Sabbath. They all knew, or thought they knew, that those who don't keep the Sabbath are sinners, and no sinner could perform such miracles. Others argued that the miracle itself was a sign from God, and God would not give such signs to sinners. And "a division arose among them" (John 9:16). They then asked the healed beggar what he thought about Jesus, to which he witnessed, "He is a prophet" (John 9:17).

The religious leaders did not believe the story so they called upon the parents of the healed beggar and asked them to confirm the identity of their son who had been born blind, and to inquire from them how he could now see. The parents said that they didn't know how it had happened, and that they should ask their son, who was of age and could speak for himself. Here John (9:22) inserted a parenthetical comment:

> "(His parents said these things because they feared the Jews, for the Jews had already agreed that if anyone should confess Jesus to be Christ, he was to be put out of the synagogue.)"

Take a moment to recount where we are in this story. Jesus healed a man born blind with spit and dirt, and now the religious leaders determined that anyone who confessed that Jesus is the Christ would be thrown out of the synagogue. And that is why the parents deflected the question back to their son: "He is of age; ask him" (John 9:23). It sounds like we are in the midst of a trial, with testimony and rebuttal.

> "So for the second time they called the man who had been blind and said to him, 'Give glory to God. We know that this man is a sinner.' He answered, 'Whether he is a sinner I do not know. One thing I do know, that though I was blind, now I see'" (John 9:24-25).

The man was careful to only testify to what he actually knew—his healing. He did not testify that Jesus was the Christ. So the religious leaders pressed him further:

> "What did he do to you? How did he open your eyes?" (John 9:26).

And he answered:

"I have told you already, and you would not listen. Why do you want to hear it again? Do you also want to become his disciples?" (John 9: 27).

Clearly, this story is not about a man born blind who was healed by Jesus. The story is much larger than that. The healing serves as a mere pretext for this larger story about Jesus.

The religious leaders were incensed that the man had suggested that they might want to become disciples of Jesus! And they reviled him, calling *him* a disciple of Jesus, and touting their own faithfulness to Moses. They could trust Moses, but Jesus was an unknown and therefore not trustworthy.

The healed beggar was amazed that they confessed that they did not know anything about Jesus, and yet it was Jesus who had opened the beggar's eyes. In other words, here was Jesus performing bonafide miracles, and the teaching of the Scriptures was that such miracles could only be performed by God's prophets. Such miracles were proof of the credibility of God's prophets. Yet, the religious leaders did not recognize this biblical fact. The healed beggar then gave his testimony:

> "We know that God does not listen to sinners, but if anyone is a worshiper of God and does his will, God listens to him. Never since the world began has it been heard that anyone opened the eyes of a man born blind" (John 9: 31-32).

Whether Jesus was a prophet or not, he did not know. But he knew for a fact that God was with Him! He could no more deny that than he could deny his own restored sight. He had been blind, but now he could see—and Jesus was the man responsible!

> "They answered him, 'You were born in utter sin, and would you teach us?' And they cast him out" (John 9:34).

Jesus heard that they had cast him out, and He sought him out to ask him if he believed in the Son of Man. Did he believe in the promised Messiah of the Old Testament? The beggar said that he did, but wanted to know who the Messiah was, so he could believe more fully.

> "Jesus said to him, 'You have seen him, and it is he who is speaking to you'" (John 9:37).

To which the beggar confessed his belief and worshiped the Lord. This confession of the once-blind beggar provided the end of the story about his healing. And with the full story now a matter of public record, Jesus could provide the central lesson of the story. There are a lot of lessons that come out of this story, but the main lesson was so important that Jesus wanted to make it perfectly clear.

> "Jesus said, 'For judgment I came into this world, that those who do not see may see, and those who see may become blind'" (John 9:39)

Clearly, this is not a story about the healing of a man born blind. It's a story about the light of Christ coming into the world, and how His light both illuminates and occludes. It's a story about the light of Christ, God's long promised Messiah, coming to the Second Temple culture of ancient Israel, and about God's judgment that leads to both salvation and damnation.

When the religious leaders heard about this larger lesson that Jesus was applying to this beggar, they were again incensed. And they asked if He meant that they were also blind.

> "Jesus said to them, 'If you were blind, you would have no guilt; but now that you say, "We see," your guilt remains'" (John 9:41).

Their denial of their own blindness convicted them of being blind to Jesus, blind to the teachings of their own Bible, and blind to what was happening right in front of them. Their denial of Jesus amounted to the denial of God and of God's mission to the world.

The Good Shepherd

Thus ends chapter 9. Chapter 10 opens with Jesus' teaching about the Good Shepherd, which stands as a further condemnation of the religious leaders. Furthering the divide, Jesus said, "All who came before me are thieves and robbers" (John 10:8). At the conclusion of teaching on the Good Shepherd we find this note about the continuation of the story of the man born blind:

> "There was again a division among the Jews because of these words. Many of them said, 'He has a demon, and is insane; why listen to him?' Others said, 'These are not the words of one who is oppressed by a demon. Can a demon open the eyes of the blind?'" (John 10:19-21).

And immediately following this, Jesus began to teach that He and the Father are One. Just as the religious leaders had previously been concerned about the claims regarding Jesus' Messiahship, so these same concerns are woven into John 10. The larger issue is whether or not Jesus is the Son of God (or Man or God's Messiah). The resolution of this issue only comes through personal insight, through *seeing* that it is true. This issue continued to trouble Jerusalem until Jesus left in order to avoid His arrest. So He went

> "across the Jordan to the place where John had been baptizing at first, and there he remained. And many came to him. And they said, 'John did no sign, but everything that John said about this man was true.' And many believed in him there" (John 10:40-42).

Resurrection

Lazarus: Dead and Alive

"Now when Jesus came, he found that Lazarus had already been in the tomb four days. Bethany was near Jerusalem, about two miles off, and many of the Jews had come to Martha and Mary to console them concerning their brother. So when Martha heard that Jesus was coming, she went and met him, but Mary remained seated in the house. Martha said to Jesus, 'Lord, if you had been here, my brother would not have died. But even now I know that whatever you ask from God, God will give you.' Jesus said to her, 'Your brother will rise again.' Martha said to him, 'I know that he will rise again in the resurrection on the last day.' Jesus said to her, 'I am the resurrection and the life. Whoever believes in me, though he die, yet shall he live, and everyone who lives and believes in me shall never die. Do you believe this?' She said to him, 'Yes, Lord; I believe that you are the Christ, the Son of God, who is coming into the world.'" —John 11:17-27

Chapter 10 is a continuation of the story of the man born blind. The culmination of that story is the realization that Jesus is God's long-awaited Messiah, the Son of God (or Man, God's Messiah). This is what the man born blind was led to *see*. And as chapter 9 closes we find Jesus accusing the Jewish leaders of being blind—spiritually blind to the very Scriptures that they claim to honor. In chapter 10 Jesus identifies Himself as the Good Shepherd (John 10:1-18). Pointing out that Jesus was not speaking literally, John added parenthetically,

"This figure of speech Jesus used with them, but they did not understand what he was saying to them" (John 10:6).

Remember that the once-blind man had been taken to court because he witnessed to the miraculous healing of his sight by Jesus. He simply spoke the truth, that Jesus had healed him, and he was thrown out of the Synagogue. And according to John 4:1, "Jesus was making and baptizing more disciples than John." John was either in prison or had been killed, and Jesus was recruiting John's disciples. This context means that Jesus' teaching had been quite successful. People were flocking to Him, to the Good Shepherd. At the conclusion of His teaching on the Good Shepherd,

"There was again a division among the Jews because of these words" (John 10:19).

The next scene opens at the Feast of Dedication, in the colonnade of Solomon, part of the Temple. It was a holy day so there would have been a lot of people there. The Jewish leaders gathered around Jesus and asked if He was the Christ, God's Messiah.

"Jesus answered them, 'I told you, and you do not believe. The works that I do in my Father's name bear witness about me, but you do not believe because you are not among my sheep. My sheep hear my voice, and I know them, and they follow me. I give them eternal life, and they will never perish, and no one will snatch them out of my hand. My Father, who has given them to me, is greater than all, and no one is able to snatch them out of the Father's hand. I and the Father are one'" (John 10:25-30).

Upon hearing this,

"The Jews picked up stones again to stone him" (John 10:31).

But they were unable. So they sought to arrest Him, but he escaped and went across the Jordan, "and many believed in Him there" (John 10:42).

The point is that chapter 10 is a continuation of the story of the man born blind in chapter 9. As I said previously, that story is not about the healing of a blind beggar, but is about the blindness of Jewish leaders.

Chapter 11 opens with the story of Lazarus. Mary and Martha told Jesus that Lazarus was ill. And Jesus responded much as He had at the beginning of the story of the man born blind.

> "But when Jesus heard it he said, 'This illness does not lead to death. It is for the glory of God, so that the Son of God may be glorified through it'" (John 11:4).

Again, the unfolding story of Lazarus would be much like the story of the man born blind, in that the story of Lazarus wasn't really about Lazarus any more than the story of the man born blind was the story of a blind beggar. The story of the man born blind quickly escalated into a major conflict with the religious leaders. We should expect something similar with the story of Lazarus.

Jesus wasn't concerned about Lazarus because Lazarus had an important role to play regarding the revelation of God's glory through Jesus Christ. The elements of this story seem to be thrown together a bit haphazardly. Mary and Martha wanted Jesus to go attend Lazarus, but Jesus was not interested and delayed His trip to see Lazarus by an additional two days, which did not please Mary and Martha. When the disciples found out where Lazarus was they registered their concern about the trip.

> "Rabbi, the Jews were just now seeking to stone you, and are you going there again?" (John 11:8).

Jesus answered cryptically, contrasting day and night, and how the the light of the world can keep people from stumbling. He ended by noting that Lazarus had "fallen asleep" and He was going to "awaken him" (John 11:11). John then added another parenthetical comment about some confusion about Lazarus being asleep or dead. Jesus responded,

> "Lazarus has died, and for your sake I am glad that I was not there, so that you may believe. But let us go to him" (John 11:15-16).

When they all finally arrived, Lazarus had been in the tomb for four days. Dead for four days! Martha went out to meet Jesus on the road, to upbraid Jesus for delaying His visit and allowing Lazarus to die. She was clearly angry at Jesus. Nonetheless, she shared her faith, saying,

> "I know that whatever you ask from God, God will give you" (John 11:22).

Jesus assured her that Lazarus would "rise again" (John 11:23). To which Martha replied,

> "I know that he will rise again in the resurrection on the last day" (John 11:24).

Belief in a general resurrection at the end of history was common among the Jews, and that was what Martha referred to. But that was not what Jesus had in mind as He answered her.

> "I am the resurrection and the life. Whoever believes in me, though he die, yet shall he live, and everyone who lives and believes in me shall never die. Do you believe this?" (John 11:25-26).

When they arrived, this scene with Martha was repeated with Mary, who also upbraided Jesus for being late. At that point Jesus found them all in tears, weeping for the death of Lazarus. Remember that Jesus had told them not to worry about Lazarus because he had an important role to play in the unfolding story of God's glory. He had assured them that Lazarus would not die until he had completed that role. So when Jesus found them all in tears over Lazarus' death, He

> "was deeply moved in his spirit and greatly troubled" (John 11:33).

When Jesus saw Lazarus lying in death He wept. But He did not weep for Lazarus. He wept for those who thought that Lazarus was lost to them. He wept because of their faithlessness in Him. Some of the Jews were impressed with Jesus' love for Lazarus, but others murmured,

> "Could not he who opened the eyes of the blind man also have kept this man from dying?" (John 11:37).

Here we see that the story of the man born blind is linked to the story of Lazarus. The greater story continues to unfold for those who have eyes to see and ears to hear.

The story of Lazarus is a kind of premonition about Jesus' own impending resurrection, and the circumstances are very similar. They arrived at the tomb, and Jesus told them to remove the stone that blocked the entrance. Martha was concerned that doing so would expose them to the stench of death, for Lazarus had been in the tomb for four days. Jesus replied to her,

"Did I not tell you that if you believed you would see the glory of God?" (John 11:40).

Jesus would not be distracted from His mission as He reminded her of that mission, because it involved Lazarus. Lazarus was the means of delivery for God's message to the world. So they removed the stone and Jesus lifted up His eyes and said,

"Father, I thank you that you have heard me. I knew that you always hear me, but I said this on account of the people standing around, that they may believe that you sent me" (John 11:41-42).

When Jesus commanded Lazarus to come out of the tomb, he came out, still bound in his burial clothes. Lazarus had been raised from death by the Word of the Lord. It was a miracle! And what was the point? What was the purpose? How did Lazarus serve the glory of God? Jesus told them plainly, the miracles of Jesus were given so

"that they may believe that you sent me" (John 11:42).

This was the same point given for the healing of man born blind. These stories, these miracles were not about the once-blind beggar or the once-dead Lazarus. They were about the glory of God being manifest in the person of Jesus Christ.

The water into wine, the woman at the well, the official's son, the pool of Bethesda, the feeding of the hungry, the walking on the water, the healing of the blind, and the resurrection of Lazarus all served the same purpose: to reveal that Jesus Christ is the Messiah of God! Glory, hallelujah!

Alphabetical Index

Adam..........................3, 178
adultery............................49
age segmented education. 34
Alexander Jannaeus.........178
amen......53, 61, 66, 141, 157
Andrew...........................116
angel................................39
antisemitism.....................88
assurance........................171
astheneō.........................106
authority......64, 74, 145, 150
authority of God................54
authority, central.............168
authority, transferred......152
authority, undermine......150
bad habits.........................41
barley.....................116, 122
belief................................63
belief and will...................63
believing on....................148
Bethesdā.........................106
Bethlehem........................30
beyond human reach........55
beyond what we know...137
Bible................................83
Bible study.......................67
blind faith........109, 113, 122
blinded by God................163
blinding the sighted........181
blindness................175, 186
blindness as denial..........181
blindness. purpose of......176
bread from heaven..........158
brokenness........................69
Calvinism and Arminianism
....155
Capernaum......133, 136, 140
charismania......................82
charity........................42, 49
chicken-and-the-egg......165
childish attachments.........81
Christ's faith.....................22
Christ's purpose................97
common sense................137
communion liturgy.........126
compassion......................80
confession.................89, 161
conscience......................100
corresponding
responsibilities..................93
crowds............106, 133, 149
culpability.......................159
cultural indoctrination......98
current events...................93
damnation...................61, 64
damnation of indecision. 145
darśana..............................2
David..............................150
death experiences.............73
depravity..........................96
discernment......................63
discrimination..................13
doctrine............................33
domesticated Jesus............87
doomed..........................169
dual nature.....................125
dual nature of Christ..........4
dunamis.............................3
ears to hear.......................66
easier to be sick................42
economic lesson.............132
economics.......................110
education.........................34
Elijah.......................78, 123
embarrassment.................25
end times........................151
enslaved humanity...........44
eternal life........17, 64, 72, 83
eternal values.................143
Evangelicalism..................34
evangelism...........14, 22, 142
evidence...........................78
ex niliho.........................123
exaggerate........................20
exaggeration.....................14
expectations.....................44
faith.................................46
faith in God......................63
faith, lack of...................142
false hope.........................67

false teaching..................92
family-centered evangelism
....................................33
fashionable styles.............143
feelings..............................43
fireman..............................98
First Commandment.........56
forgiveness................88, 101
foundation for the gospel. 25
four witnesses....................77
free will...........................170
freedom...........................166
Galilee......................30, 105
George Washington..........82
get a life............................48
glory of God...................189
God asks too much,........171
God's backwardness..........24
God's economy.......110, 124
God's order......................126
God's presence................131
God's purpose...................44
God's timing...................123
God's unwillingness..........85
God's will................16, 165
good intentions...............144
good news.........................91
goodness...........................91
gospel preaching...............25
Graham, Billy.................152
grass........................117, 122
greater miracle........119, 125
half a story......................137
half-way measure..............97
half-way measures...........137
healing...........33, 70, 80, 178
healing through obedience
....................................44
heaven......................62, 65
heavenly entrance exam...83
Hezekiah.........................178
historical sign..................131
history.............................115
Hodge, Charles................153
Holy Spirit.....41, 44, 54, 63,
65, 70, 81, 99, 132, 171
holy water.........................48
homosexuality..................90
honor....................30, 58, 95

humanity...........................72
humility..........................133
idolatry..............70, 166, 169
ignorance........................162
impossible.......................137
India..................................2
indignation.......................41
inoculation......................161
interpretation...........134, 148
invalid..............................41
itching ears.....................159
Jacob's ladder......................3
Jerusalem..........................31
Jesus wept.......................188
Jesus' accusation..............105
Jesus' intention.................79
John the Baptist................78
judgment...................64, 71
justification......................89
Kingdom of God 18, 33, 65,
72
Lazarus.....................73, 187
lifestyles............................42
literary genius...................16
living a lie........................50
local church.....150, 153, 167
madness..........................167
magic...46, 48, 109, 118, 122
manna.............................158
marketplace....................124
marvel..............................71
mass media.....................151
medical industry...............47
mercy...............................38
Messiah...........................158
Messianic predictions..33, 49
miracle.....43, 65, 70, 72, 80,
101, 118, 122, 125, 131
miraclē............................107
miracle of sharing............124
miracles and doctrine........34
miracles, greater and lesser
....................................80
miraculous healing....41, 186
miraculous intervention....65
misunderstanding....160, 163
misunderstood the prophets
....................................97
mob mentality.................149

modern church..................90
money.............................115
money-changers..............107
monotheism......................55
moral decay....................166
moral failure...............96, 99
moralistic stories...............93
Moses.........97, 136, 157, 180
multiculturalism................55
mutual accountability
relationship...................169
natural explanation 122, 125,
135
natural order...................114
new eyes..................119, 123
norm................................73
obedience 48, 58, 62, 66, 95,
165
obedience of faith..............47
object of faith....................64
occupied.....................43, 48
old time preachers............23
once saved always saved. 171
opposing perspectives.....170
ordinary becoming
extraordinary..................8
ordinary means...............114
outward manifestation......83
overlooked......................115
Passover..........................107
pastoral charisma..............34
peace................................24
personal experience...21, 83,
168
personal relationship. 81, 152
perspectivalism................155
Peter.................................13
Pharisees...........................97
Philip......................108, 115
pity...................................38
political correctness...........89
political event.................132
political power..................48
politically motivated.......132
Pool of Bethesda.........38, 40
poverty...............................5
poverty of language...........54
preacher's responsibility....93
predestination..166, 168, 170

premature invitation..........22
preservation of the saints 171
proof...........................65, 148
providence.....109, 114, 119, 122, 126
provisions..........................107
psychologists and educators 23
psychology........................91
purpose............................167
regeneration....30, 74, 80, 82
religious patronage............48
repentance...................82, 91
reserve judgment.............137
resistance is futile.............101
resurrection...57, 65, 71, 80, 188
reversal of the normal..........7
revival..............................127
righteous indignation........32
ritual..................................8
Sabbath................47, 50, 179
sacrifices...........................97
salvation. .24, 58, 61, 74, 88, 132, 145, 171
salvation and damnation. 181
salvation decision..............98
salvationv..........................82
Samaria...................18, 30
Samaritan 12, 16, 19, 21, 25, 31, 33
Sanhedrin........................106
sarcasm............................158
Satan............70, 80, 119, 163
Satan. blindness...............176
Saul..................................150

saving faith.......................148
school prayer.....................90
science..............................148
Sea of Galilee...................133
second exodus..................136
Second Temple culture...181
self reliance........................63
self-esteem..........23, 141, 168
self-professed Christians. 107
self-reliance.....................161
self-sufficient.....................70
semeion............................3, 5
sentimentality....................43
sheep gate..........................39
shepherding....................150
signs and wonders........34, 46
sin. .23, 49, 69, 90, 100, 132, 176
slain in the Spirit...............82
social media....................152
Son of God. .54, 80, 182, 185
Son of Man.......................71
soul..............................15, 81
spiritual apathȳ................106
spiritual blindness...........160
spiritual death...................67
spiritual harvest.................17
spiritual journey..............137
spiritual poverty................66
success..............................90
Sunday School................161
supernatural.....46, 113, 118, 133, 136, 145
supernatural explanation 122, 125
supernatural intervention 70, 124

superstars..........................152
superstition 7, 37, 44, 46, 48, 51, 159
Temple drainage system...38
Temple, Second..................7
Ten Commandments.......63, 159, 176
testimony...........................22
testing Philip...................108
thankfulness....................141
Thomas...................160, 162
too busy...........................163
Trinity...................54, 70, 74
unbelievers........................78
understanding.................169
unexpected......................177
unites and divides..............74
unity..................................74
universal emancipation.....13
universal salvation.............57
vicious cycle......................70
voluntary...........................62
walking on the sea..........135
walking the walk.............135
walking the walk,.............46
wedding................32, 46, 71
willing..............................42
willing to be wrong........162
wisdom.............................18
witness..............................20
works-righteousness 47, 144, 148
worldly business................47
worldly concerns.............143
worship...........................167

Scripture Index

Genesis 28:12......................3

Exodus 16:15...................157
Exodus 18:25...................150
Exodus 20:3.......................55
Exodus 20:5.....................176
Exodus 20:12.....................58

Numbers 11:5...................153

1 Kings 17:12-16.............123

Job 28:28.........................163

Psalm 14:1.......................168
Psalm 139:6.......................55

Proverbs 12:15.................168
Proverbs 14:12..........152, 169

Isaiah 55:8.......................168
Isaiah 64:6.......................101

Jeremiah 4:22...................168
Jeremiah 6-8.....................24
Jeremiah 20:12...................40
Jeremiah 32:17.................119

Ezekiel 13:2.....................168

Zephaniah 1:17.................176

Matthew 3:13–17..................6
Matthew 3:3...............78, 119
Matthew 4:4......15, 115, 119
Matthew 5:4.......................26
Matthew 6:10.....................64
Matthew 7:21..144, 145, 171
Matthew 7:21-13................83
Matthew 7:22-23................56
Matthew 10:14...................21
Matthew 10:28...........15, 163
Matthew 12:26-28..............80
Matthew 14:15.........108, 116

Matthew 14:23.................132
Matthew 25:21...................95
Matthew 26:41...................41

Mark 1:9–11.......................6
Mark 6:36........................116
Mark 6:46........................132

Luke 3:21–23......................6
Luke 2:21-38.......................5
Luke 9:12........................116
Luke 15:24........................65
Luke 16:31........................73
Luke 24:19........................30

John 1:29–33......................6
John 1:19..........................78
John 1:50............................2
John 2:3-4...........................6
John 2:4......................32, 46
John 2:11..........................32
John 2:14-15.....................31
John 2:18..........................33
John 2:23..........................31
John 3:2............................79
John 3:3............................73
John 3:16........................162
John 3:18..........................81
John 3:22..........................78
John 4:1..........................186
John 4:20..........................31
John 4:45..........................31
John 4:45..........................31
John 4:46-54.....................46
John 4:48..........................32
John 5:3............................46
John 5:8..........................135
John 5:19-47...................161
John 5:35..........................79
John 5:37-46.....................89
John 5:39..........................85
John 6:23........................140
John 6:66..................34, 132
John 7:16..........................64

John 8:11..........................49
John 8:47..........................82
John 9:3..........................176
John 9:4-5.......................177
John 9:5..........................177
John 9:6..........................177
John 9:7..........................178
John 9:9..........................178
John 9:16........................179
John 9:17........................179
John 9:22........................179
John 9:23........................179
John 9:23........................179
John 9:24-25...................179
John 9:26........................180
John 9: 27......................180
John 9: 31-32..................180
John 9:34........................180
John 9:37........................181
John 9:39........................181
John 9:41........................181
John 10:1-18...................185
John 10:6........................186
John 10:8........................182
John 10:19......................186
John 10:19-21.................182
John 10:25........................79
John 10:25-30.................186
John 10:31......................186
John 10:35......................166
John 10:40-42.................182
John 10:42......................186
John 11:4........................187
John 11:8........................187
John 11:11......................187
John 11:15-16.................187
John 11:22......................188
John 11:24......................188
John 11:25-26.................188
John 11:33......................188
John 11:37......................188
John 11:40......................189
John 11:41-42.................189
John 11:42......................189

John 14:5............160, 162	1 Corinthians 1:18-19.....176	1 Thessalonians 5:18........140
John 14:6..........................162	1 Corinthians 1:22.............34	
John 14:10............................64	1 Corinthians 1:23.............88	2 Timothy 3:16...............166
John 15:24...........................79	1 Corinthians 2:3...............41	2 Timothy 4:3.................159
John 17:15...........................15	1 Corinthians 2:14...........176	
John 20:15.............................6	1 Corinthians 3:1.............168	Hebrews 11:1..............73, 83
	1 Corinthians 11:2...........151	James 1:21..........................82
Acts 1:8..............................171		James 3:1-12....................178
Acts 2:37...........................145		James 4:2............................88
Acts 2:41.............................66	2 Corinthians 4:4.............163	
Acts 10:11-15......................13	2 Corinthians 4:4.............177	
Acts 16:30.........................145		1 Peter 3:7..........................40
	Galatians 3:3.....................168	
Romans 1:5.......................171	Galatians 5:1.......................13	2 Peter 3:17......................151
Romans 1:21.....................168		
Romans 3:10.......................57	Ephesians 1:4....................166	Jude 1:4.............................151
Romans 11:25...................163		
Romans 14:10.....................65	Colossians 3:17................140	Revelation 6:6..................117
Romans 16:26...................171		Revelation 12:9................151

www.ingramcontent.com/pod-product-compliance
Lightning Source LLC
LaVergne TN
LVHW051518070426
835507LV00023B/3174